Praise for

Main Street Entrepreneur

Michael Glauser's *Main Street Entrepreneur* is filled with real learnings from the trenches of startups and delivers a complete tool box for entrepreneurs to start and build their own businesses. Glauser's success as an entrepreneur, along with the insights and learnings of another 100 entrepreneurs, gives the book enormous credibility and gravitas. This is a timely and relevant book that is written in an immediately applicable way—and for that I highly recommend it!

—Stephen M. R. Covey, Author of *The Speed of Trust*, Coauthor of *Smart Trust*

Technology is eliminating jobs in nearly every industry at an ever increasing pace. In the near future, more of us will have to become entrepreneurs and create our own jobs. During his 4,000 mile bike ride across America, Michael Glauser, developed a clear road map anyone can follow to build a successful company. His book will help you create the life of your dreams. It's time to get started.

—Daven Michaels, Author of *Outsource Smart*, Founder and CEO of 123Employee

Every year we mentor thousands of people all over the world who are trying to rise out of poverty by starting their own business. The key concepts taught in *Main Street Entrepreneur* are the exact principles people need to implement to be successful. I highly recommend this book to anyone who wants to start a business and achieve their dreams.

—Mark L. Petersen, President and CEO of Mentors International

Make no mistake, the American Dream is alive. People are merging their livelihood and lifestyle by doing what they love while living where they want. In *Main Street Entrepreneur* you will meet remarkable entrepreneurs and discover the key principles for achieving your dream. A must read for anyone seeking more freedom, security, and happiness!

—Judy Robinett, Startup Funding Expert, Author of *How to Be a Power Connector*

Michael Glauser shares the secrets to success that entrepreneurs across the country have used to enjoy the American Dream. His nine keys will help any ambitious soul achieve and sustain success. Building a successful business, and lifestyle, just became easier with *Main Street Entrepreneur*.

—Roger Connors, Cofounder of Partners In Leadership, Author of *The Oz Principle*

Glauser takes us on a literal ride to the near future where the small sole proprietors create the business future that multinational corporations once controlled. An essential read to help you succeed in the post-capitalist economy of the near future.

—Geoffrey Colon, Communications Designer at Microsoft, Author of *Disruptive Marketing*

I love Michael Glauser's bike trip across America as an analogy for business development. As a three time Hawaii Ironman finisher and college swimmer I can attest that the purpose and passion necessary to succeed as an athlete are precisely the same disciplines that can produce success in all aspects of one's life, whether it's business, health or relationships. There are always going to be bumps and pot holes in the road. Glauser is spot on when he says that keeping your purpose in focus is the most important thing to get you to the finish line.

—Howard Liebowitz, MD, FACEP, Director of Liebowitz Longevity Medicine, Foremost Anti-Aging Medicine and Hormone Specialist

The people I meet who are not executives all dream of starting their own company. But they don't because they don't know how and can't see themselves in the lore of multi-billion dollar success. Finally, the masses have a roadmap to attain a more Main Street success.

—Mark Cook, Director of O.C. Tanner Institute, author of *Sales Blazers*, Adjunct Professor of Entrepreneurship

I started my first business at age 15 and have run my sixth for almost 30 years now. Oh, what heartache and sleepless nights I could have saved myself if I had only had Michael Glauser's insightful book from the beginning! What a fun and easy read to experience his cycling adventure right along with the interesting and wise people he met on his bold journey! I recommend this book big time.

—Wendy Keller, Author of *Secrets of Successful Negotiation for Women*

MAIN STREET ENTREPRENEUR

BUILD YOUR DREAM COMPANY DOING WHAT YOU LOVE WHERE YOU LIVE

MICHAEL GLAUSER

Entrepreneur PRESS®

Entrepreneur Press, Publisher
Cover Design: Andrew Welyczko
Production and Composition: Eliot House Productions

Library of Congress Cataloging-in-Publication Data
Names: Glauser, Michael J., author.
Title: Main street entrepreneur : build your dream company doing what you love where you live / by Michael J. Glauser.
Description: Irvine, California : Entrepreneur Press, [2016]
Identifiers: LCCN 2015051285 | ISBN 978-1-59918-590-3 (hardback) | ISBN 1-59918-590-3 (hardback)
Subjects: LCSH: Small business. | Small business—Location. | New business enterprises. | Entrepreneurship. | Success in business. | BISAC: BUSINESS & ECONOMICS / Entrepreneurship.
Classification: LCC HD2341 .G52 2016 | DDC 658.1/1—dc23
LC record available at http://lccn.loc.gov/2015051285

Printed in the United States of America

20 19 18 17 16 10 9 8 7 6 5 4 3 2 1

Contents

PROLOGUE

A New Career Path for Our Changing Economy

I never imagined receiving that call—the one from the CEO of a publicly traded company in Toronto, Canada.

"Mike, I want to talk with you about buying your company," he said.

"I am flattered, but it's not for sale," I replied.

"Every company is for sale for the right terms and conditions," he retorted. "I think you are going to like what we're doing in the industry." So I told him he was welcome to come and visit us.

A week later he showed up with his executive team at our offices in Salt Lake City. They spent two days poring over our financial statements and company documents. At the end of the second day, the CEO came into my office and placed a formal offer on my desk. I glanced at the number and knew it was too low. I also knew my board would never accept this price. I told him this, and he said, "Well, write a number you would accept at the bottom of the page." I increased his offer by 30 percent and handed the paper back to him. I watched as his eyes widened in surprise.

"Let me think about this tonight," he said, "and I'll get back to you tomorrow."

The next morning he came into my office and said, "We will pay the full price you are asking, on two conditions." *Great*, I thought. *Here come the deal killers*. Since I wasn't trying to sell the company, I didn't want to haggle over his terms.

"First, we don't need you in the company. We will move the office to Dallas, where we have our own team." No problem. I had thought about what I would do if I ever sold the company, and had already decided I didn't want to run something I no longer owned.

"Second," he said in a very serious tone, "you have to take cash." I couldn't believe it. I had discussed the sale with my board members the day before. Everyone was open to an offer at the price I had suggested, but no one wanted to take stock in his company. So I held a look of consternation as long as I could and then said, "OK, I think we have a deal."

A few months later the transaction was final, and I left the company. I was now free for my next adventure. After contemplating my passions, values, skills, and experience, I made a strong commitment to spend the rest of my career helping people create their own jobs, build their own organizations, and live their own dreams—just as I had done.

This book is part of that commitment. It presents nine powerful keys to help you build your own successful business. These keys were gleaned from interviews I conducted with 100 small-town entrepreneurs during a remarkable bicycle ride from the west coast of Oregon to the east coast of Virginia. I rode 4,000 miles in 45 days, spent 246 hours on a bike seat, climbed 155,000 vertical feet, and visited more than 100 cities across the country. Although I weathered hail and snow in Montana, unrelenting head winds in Kansas, a hard crash in Kentucky, and torrential rains in Virginia, my journey was mostly delightful sunny days, nights with stars as bright as diamonds, and a glorious homage to American ingenuity. I can honestly say it was one of the most amazing experiences of my life so far.

The best part of my bizarre and beautiful escapade was the remarkable entrepreneurs I discovered. These innovative business builders are living in attractive places and flying under the radar of the media. Take Benny and Julie Benson. They design, build, and operate biomass power plants all over the country from their corporate office in Sisters, Oregon—a beautiful town of a little more than 2,000 people. Gail and Will Williams have built a thriving sewing company on a gorgeous ridge in northern Idaho that manufactures seat cushions for 600 ski resorts worldwide. Jason Kintzler developed a disruptive technology in his hometown of Lander, Wyoming, that has transformed the public relations industry; his clients include PepsiCo, Walmart, Budweiser, and 50,000 other businesses. And then there's Hank Viccellio. He creates and ships his elegant "wearable art" around the world from his shop on the vibrant waterfront of Yorktown, Virginia.

These extraordinary role models have a great deal to teach us about building a purpose-driven business, meeting important community needs, developing a supporting cast, using a host of resources other than money, working with a zealous tenacity, giving mind-boggling customer service, diversifying revenue streams, giving back to the broader community, and living life joyfully. The important lessons taught by these entrepreneurs will benefit you a great deal if you want to:

- Start and operate your own new company
- Keep your job but diversify your income
- Make your current business more sustainable
- Grow your existing company to a higher level
- Do what you love for the rest of your life
- Create the lifestyle of your dreams

The nine keys to success presented in this book are the very foundation of grass-roots business building; they are the "differences that make the difference" between success and failure when starting, operating, and growing a company. Not everyone can build a Facebook, Google, or eBay, but I believe anyone with passion and tenacity can do what the entrepreneurs I met are doing. In the chapters that follow, you will learn how to achieve your own dreams—and you won't need a 30-page business plan, you won't need venture capital, you won't need to take giant risks, and you won't need an exit strategy. All you need to do is implement the nine keys to success. Before proceeding, though, let me tell you about my own adventures in entrepreneurship.

My Entrepreneurial Journey

My passion for entrepreneurship started when I was in college. I wanted to learn how to build great companies that were satisfying places for people to work. My quest for this knowledge quickly propelled me through three degrees, including a Ph.D. from Purdue University, before I was 30. In the 1980s, business schools did not offer degrees in entrepreneurship, so I pieced together an exciting interdisciplinary program in organizational studies. While working on this degree, I only had to take one class I didn't love—statistics—but it taught me a great deal about collecting and interpreting data.

After earning my doctorate, I walked into my first MBA class as "Dr. Glauser" and wrote my name on the board. When I turned around to face the class, I realized I was the youngest person in the room by nearly ten years. The students were full-time managers and executives in a part-time MBA program. While I was clearly on top of the academic heap with my Ph.D., every student in the class beat me in terms of experience. I knew a lot about organizational theory; they knew a lot about organizations. Though I managed to impress them with my intellectual bravado, I felt I was masquerading as a business authority.

I continued to teach for a few more years, but I knew I had to leave the safe harbor of academics and do the real thing. I had studied organizations and taught about organizational theory, and now I wanted to build organizations. I needed to prove that I could practice what I was preaching, so I left higher education and jumped into the world of starting and building companies.

My first venture was a management consulting practice. I had numerous clients: large and small, national and international, everything from new startups to colossal corporations. I consulted on a variety of topics, including strategic planning, market research, corporate restructuring, and management development—anything I could sell. I helped executive teams create and implement expansion plans, trained worldwide sales forces, taught Catholic nuns how to administer schools, assisted geologists looking for an ore body, promoted team building in an underground mine, and helped morticians provide better service to grieving families.

My consulting experience taught me how to grow and develop a wide variety of organizations. But I wasn't creating independent value beyond my own activities. I wanted to build a business that was bigger than myself: I wanted to develop innovative products, create jobs, hire team members, build a great culture, and grow equity in a company. After exploring a number of options, my wife Mary and I had the concept: We would combine my skills in business strategy with her training in health and nutrition and launch a business in the specialty foods industry. Over the next few years we created a full line of frozen dessert products that had no fat and low calories, and yet tasted fantastic. We sold these products to wholesale customers in the food-service industry and retailed them through outlets in malls, strip centers, grocery stores, stadiums, and arenas.

The Canadian company that bought our business had raised millions of dollars on the Toronto Stock Exchange. The executives were on a buying spree to acquire specialty food companies in the United States. They had recently purchased Bresler's Ice Cream, I Can't Believe It's Yogurt!, and Java Coast Fine Coffees. They liked the tandem relationship between our wholesale distribution and our retail sales. When they purchased our company, we had hundreds of wholesale accounts, dozens of retail outlets, and more than 500 employees. By employee head count, we were in the top few percent of businesses in America.

After selling the company, I was fully committed to my new passion: to help people build their own ventures. Business schools were now teaching entrepreneurship, so I considered going back to academics. But when I reviewed the various courses that were being offered, it was obvious that academic entrepreneurship and real-world business building were not the same things. What I had just done in the field did not resemble what was being taught in the classroom at all. My conclusion was that we need to learn a lot more about what winning entrepreneurs actually do, identify their common practices, and then use these keys to teach entrepreneurship and business development. This is when I launched one of the most exciting projects of my career.

My idea was to visit, observe, and record the stories of hundreds of innovative business builders around the country. I essentially became an entrepreneurial anthropologist: walking the streets, peeking around corners, touring plants and factories, flying in company helicopters, conducting in-depth interviews, and recording everything I saw and heard. I have continued this real-world discovery process, which I call "shoe-leather research," for nearly two decades. I have collected hundreds of oral histories from extraordinary role models. I have spent time with the founders of billion-dollar companies, like Jon Huntsman Sr., who built the Huntsman Corporation, and David Neeleman, who built JetBlue and Azul Airlines. I have also hung out with the founders of much smaller lifestyle businesses like David Tibbitts, owner of Jackson Hole Whitewater, a river-running company in Wyoming, and Gregory Jacobs, one of the legendary "Bushmen" of San Francisco, who made his living scaring people at Fisherman's Wharf for nearly 20 years.

I've used the lessons I have learned from these amazing entrepreneurs to write articles, give speeches, conduct seminars, design university courses, and consult with hundreds of startup companies. I have to tell you, I love my work! Nothing is more rewarding to me than meeting inspiring role models, summarizing their stories, sharing their keys to success, and helping aspiring business builders achieve their dreams.

Why This Book Is Important

This book is a continuation of my shoe-leather field research. The entrepreneurs you are about to meet are a unique breed. They are some of the most interesting people I have ever met. These are men and women who find a community they love and then find things they love doing in that community so they can take care of themselves. They are masters at merging livelihood and lifestyle. In the process, they are building regional, national, and international companies.

So let me get to the heart of this story. It's why I took my crazy bike ride across America and why I am sharing this book with you. I believe this "Main Street" approach to building businesses will become more and more significant for a number of reasons: First, technology is replacing jobs in nearly every industry at an accelerated rate. Second, many of us want the more attractive lifestyle that smaller communities offer. And third, our buying preferences are shifting from the large conglomerates to smaller, local businesses. I believe that sharing the stories of the amazing cast of characters I discovered will provide splendid insights for addressing these changing economic trends. Let's take a few minutes and discuss each trend in a bit more detail.

Technology Is Eliminating Jobs

Science fiction writers have warned us for decades that we will become the architects of our own obsolescence, being replaced by the machines we build. This warning, often laughed off, is now becoming a reality. Every year the software and hardware we create become more and more sophisticated and capable of doing a wide variety of jobs far better than humans can. As a result, entire employment categories are being obliterated in nearly every industry, and they are not coming back. Self-checkout lines are eliminating positions in the grocery industry. Ecommerce is reducing jobs in the retail world. Robots are being increasingly used in manufacturing and other industries. Many jobs in the service sector are now being performed by computers. Online learning is replacing the traditional "brick-and-mortar" educational model. Smart cars may reduce the need for humans in the driving sector. And delivery drones may eliminate millions of jobs in the transportation industry.

The result is that large corporations need fewer employees to achieve major gains in productivity. This is a significant shift from the past century, where economic growth and job creation went hand in hand—more growth led to more jobs. Now major increases in productivity are occurring with corresponding decreases in employment opportunities. So what does this mean for our future careers? Recent studies by researchers at MIT, Oxford University, the Associated Press, the Federal Reserve Bank, and others suggest that: 1) nearly half of our occupations could become obsolete due to new technology, 2) four out of five of us will experience significant periods of unemployment during our careers, 3) new technology often leaves employees feeling disengaged and disconnected from meaningful work, and 4) job displacement due to technological acceleration will primarily impact the middle class.

You may already be experiencing the effect of this employment shift. A series of articles in *The New York Times* in 2015 about the reshaping of the American economy shows that members of the middle class are feeling increasing stress about their financial security. This middle-class anxiety is the result of fewer attractive jobs for those with higher education levels, instability of income, and failure to achieve "real incomes" beyond their parents' level. Especially troubling is the fact that the typical American family today earns 4.8 percent less than families made 25 years ago even though the costs of housing, education, and health care are increasing. Unfortunately, this trend may continue as computers, robots, and machines continue to efficiently replace jobs in nearly every industry. While we don't know exactly what jobs of the future will look like, we can probably count on more outsourcing, more contract work, more project-based opportunities, more part-time employment, and shorter employment periods. Hence, the greater need for us to create our own meaningful jobs and organizations.

Our Preference for Smaller Communities

Blow up your TV, throw away your paper
Go to the country, build you a home
Plant a little garden, eat a lot of peaches
Try and find Jesus on your own.

The dream life expressed in this witty John Prine song, "Spanish Pipedream," is alive and well in America. A 2014 survey conducted by the Pew Research Center shows that 46 percent of Americans are not happy with the place they are living, an attitude most widely held among city dwellers. When participants were asked what type of community they would prefer, 30 percent said a small town, 24 percent said a rural area, 21 percent said a suburb, and 24 percent said a city. Thus, more than half of us would prefer to live in smaller communities or rural areas.

Other studies reveal the reasons we want to move to smaller communities: better lifestyle, safer streets, lower traffic, affordable housing, a great place to raise a family, a sense of community, scenic beauty, and environmental quality. Since job opportunities are limited, employment is seldom mentioned as a reason people want to move to small towns and rural communities. So those of us who want to "blow up our TV and move to the country" need to figure out what we can do to support this choice. Ironically, the same technologies that are eliminating jobs allow us to work from anywhere: home, hotels, airports, and desirable smaller communities.

Our Preference for Small Businesses

A few years ago, my consulting team was hired by a large buying co-op that purchases and distributes products to more than 500 independently owned grocery stores. The executives were starting to buy some of the stores in their co-op and were trying to figure out what to do with these company-owned units. They hired the former president of a large grocery chain to address the opportunity. His solution was to create a new chain with a common brand, logo, design, and strategy. The CEO of the co-op hired our team to see if they were moving in the right direction. After several months of focus groups and customer surveys, the answer was clear: No one wanted the company to create a new national chain with a common name and design—and the feelings were rather strong. Customers wanted to continue patronizing local businesses where they knew the owners and employees by name. They wanted the stores to support the local Girl Scouts, soccer teams, and community fundraisers. They wanted each store to be unique and quaint, different from other stores in the area. Some people surveyed said they would not support these stores if they became another big chain. So the co-op kept all the original brands intact and even gave some store managers ownership so there would still be a local owner in the community.

Research strongly supports this anecdotal story. We love small businesses far more than we do large corporations, big box stores, and standardized chains. Studies by the Public Affairs Council during the past few years shed light on our attitudes about small versus large companies. Nearly 90 percent of those surveyed view small businesses favorably, with 53 percent giving them a "very favorable" rating. This compares to a 67 percent favorability rating for large businesses, with only 16 percent viewing them as "very favorable." In addition, nearly half of Americans say small-business owners exhibit high ethical standards; only 6 percent say the same about CEOs of large corporations. Perhaps most important, two-thirds of us would rather shop at small businesses even if the prices are slightly higher.

In some parts of the country, we are seeing a similar backlash against big box and chain stores. Zoning laws against "Formula Retail" in some cities are restricting the growth of these businesses. Along with these increasing restrictions, many cities and organizations are taking a positive approach to promoting small businesses around the country. For example, American Express launched "Small Business Saturday" in 2010 to celebrate the smaller companies on Main Street America that serve as cornerstones to our neighborhoods and communities. In addition, Goldman Sachs has allocated $500 million to its "10,000 Small Businesses" program. The goal of the program is to help existing small business owners grow their companies. Clearly, smaller businesses are capturing our hearts and our dollars.

In some ways, we are experiencing a throwback to the 19th and early 20th centuries, when people knew they had to develop skills to take care of themselves because there were no large corporations to provide long-term employment security. Based on products and services needed in their communities, people chose to become farmers, carpenters, blacksmiths, merchants, furniture makers, seamstresses, innkeepers, doctors, dentists, nurses, butchers, bakers, and candlestick makers. And most families developed multiple streams of revenue: farmer and carpenter, rancher and blacksmith, merchant and seamstress, and so on. While our changing employment landscape presents obvious challenges, it also provides an opportunity to rethink our careers.

A New Career Path

The lessons taught by the entrepreneurs in this book reveal a new approach for navigating our changing economy. This strategy includes elements from the past coupled with modern technology that allows us to live and work where we choose. The important question today is not "How do I find a job?" but rather "How do I create my own job?" To successfully answer this question, we need to view ourselves as our own unique enterprise and develop the attitude and skills to succeed. We must learn how to identify important needs in our community, develop products and services to meet those needs, build a strong network of contacts, provide astounding value to customers, cultivate multiple streams of revenue, and operate effectively in tight-knit communities—all the things winning small-town entrepreneurs do well.

Here is an example of this new career mentality from my ride across America. After a tough divorce, Kelly Harris returned home to her beloved Shenandoah Valley in Virginia to heal. She took a job with the local newspaper and bought a quaint two-bedroom bungalow on an acre of land overlooking the Blue Ridge Mountains. She started practicing massage therapy part time, a skill she had developed earlier in her career, and a few years later, she was ready to make the break. She quit her job and started a full-time massage business. She also taught piano lessons and played in a band on the side. One day she got a call from the owners of a party store who needed a clown to sing to a student at Washington and Lee University in Lexington, Virginia. This is how her next revenue stream, "K.C. the Clown," was born. In addition to dressing up as a clown, Kelly resurrected her skills as a ventriloquist, a talent she developed in her youth by using her sister as the dummy until her parents bought her a puppet. Now she performs with her puppet, "Dee-oh-Gee" the dog, at birthday parties, schools, and civic organizations. Kelly has made this life work for her for more than ten years: massage therapist, music teacher, performer, clown, and ventriloquist. "I am doing exactly what I want, where I want to be," Kelly says. "I live in my vacation spot. I have so much fun."

This new career path puts each of us at the center of our own future. I call this epicenter "My Enterprise," or "M.E." for short. I also add "LLC" because most new ventures are registered as limited liability companies, a flexible business entity that combines the tax advantages of a partnership with the liability protection of a corporation. Hence: M.E. LLC. In this new career path, you may build a primary venture, spin off a second related venture, occasionally do contract work, and start making investments to provide long-term security. Figure P–1 illustrates what your new enterprise may look like:

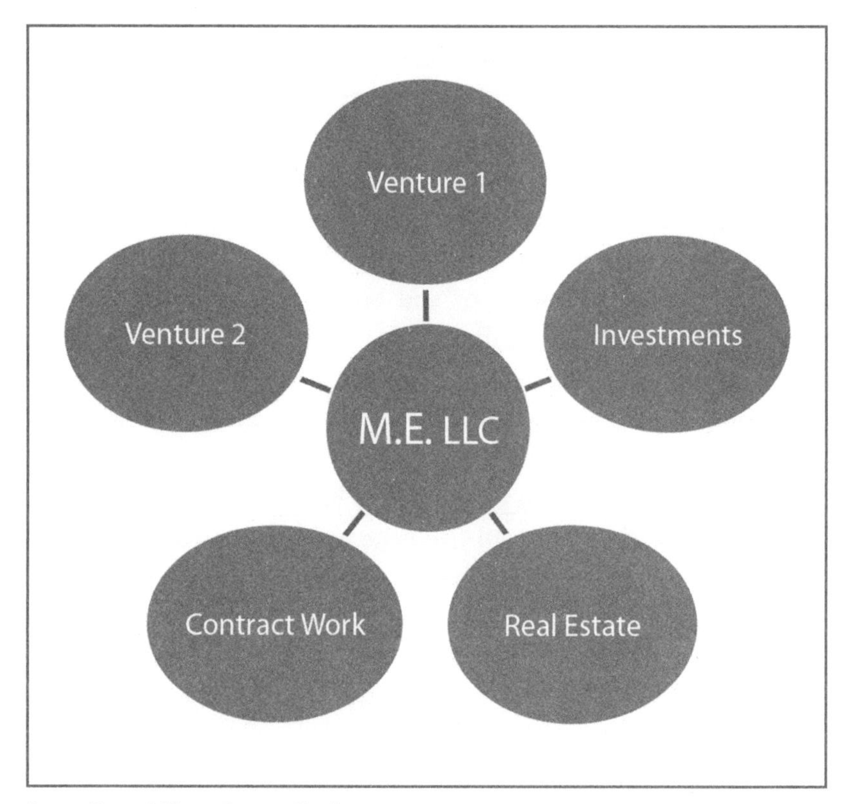

Figure P–1: **A New Career Path**

The nine keys to success that follow are your systematic road map for creating your own new enterprise. I observed them again and again in the stories I collected during my bike ride across America. While there are many things you have to do to build a company, these practices make the most difference between success and failure. The more you learn to apply them, the higher the probability that your business will first survive, and then thrive. After watching hundreds of entrepreneurs succeed, I know you can do it, too—and it can happen faster than you think.

The nine keys to success are presented in chapters 2 through 10 in this book. As you read these chapters, you will learn a great deal more about the critical practices for business building, you will see how these amazing role models apply them in their companies, and you will learn how to apply them in your own enterprise. The epilogue summarizes the overall road map to success, and you will see how easy it is to implement the things you have learned. Before outlining these key practices, let me tell you more about my amazing bike ride across America, and how I found the extraordinary entrepreneurs you are about to meet.

CHAPTER

1

Our Search for Entrepreneurs on Main Street

"This is not a business to me; I have a business so I can make jewelry. In my world, this is the greatest place I have ever been. As far as the American Dream goes, I am living it!"

—Hank Viccellio, founder of Viccellio Goldsmith & Fine Jewelry

We are bouncing on the cobblestones along the Colonial Parkway between Williamsburg and Yorktown, Virginia. We have ten more miles until we accomplish our mission: to ride our bikes from the west coast of Oregon to the east coast of Virginia and interview 100 successful small-town entrepreneurs along the way. We are going 20 miles an hour, but my mind is spinning much faster. I am reveling in a jumble of emotions: anticipation to finally see the Atlantic Ocean, elation for completing such a difficult feat, love for my teammates who joined me on the ride, awe for the remarkable people we have met along the way, and an overwhelming appreciation for such an incredible country. I have lived in America my whole life, but I haven't seen it until now.

I am also feeling sorrow that our simple and exhilarating lifestyle is ending. Each day we get up, eat a lot of food, ride our bikes for five to eight hours, interview a couple of really remarkable entrepreneurs, eat a lot more food, go to sleep in our motorhome, and then get up and do it again the next day—just like the movie *Groundhog Day*. Although we have weathered some serious storms and had a few setbacks, our escapade across the country has been the adventure of a lifetime. After 4,000 miles, 45 days of riding, and 246 hours on a bike seat, it seems as though this is all we know. Now we are nearly at the finish line.

The significance of concluding our trip on the historic Colonial Parkway is powerful. Not only is the scenery spectacular, with thick forests, rivers, bays, and canopies of trees, but it's also the place where our country began. The parkway connects three significant cities known as the Historic Triangle. Jamestown is the home of the first permanent English settlers in North America; Williamsburg was the capital of the Virginia colony from 1699 to 1780; and Yorktown is the site of the last major land battle of the Revolutionary War, the place where a ragged band of poorly fed, poorly clothed, and poorly armed freedom fighters, with the help of the French, defeated Great Britain, at the time arguably the greatest army in the world.

A mile from Yorktown I feel like a rebel soldier charging to the beach, fighting my own battle, about to win the war. We hesitate a few blocks from town, trying to decide who should lead the final assault. Our good friend Peter Foss, who joined us in Virginia, leads the way to the Victory Monument on the hill above the beach. The monument, officially named *The Monument to the Alliance and Victory*, commemorates the union between France and the colonies during the war. Without the French, who had a raging grudge against England and provided money, supplies, weapons, and a naval blockade on the York River, the rebel colonists would have surely lost the war. In addition to the colonists' alliance with France, the monument celebrates the surrender of Lord Cornwallis to George Washington. We have experienced the extraordinary outcomes that have grown from this epicenter of freedom during our coast-to-coast bicycle adventure.

The 98-foot granite monument appears incandescent in the bright afternoon sun. Standing near its base, we quietly absorb the symbolism of victory. What a perfect place to end our journey. In most countries it takes months or even years to obtain all the approvals necessary to start a new business. In America we can do it in one day. It is clear to me that the freedom we enjoy in our country plays a major role in our ability to build our dreams. I feel a rush of gratitude for those who have gone before and laid the foundation for free enterprise.

Hank Viccellio, our 100th entrepreneur, is waiting for us at his shop near the beach. He is the founder of Viccellio Goldsmith & Fine Jewelry, located in Yorktown's vibrant waterfront district. Hank grew up in Yorktown, left when he was 18, and returned nearly 30 years later to create the life of his dreams. He sells his elegant "wearable art" to people who visit Yorktown and ships his unique artistic creations all over the country. During our interview, Hank summarizes the story we have heard again and again from entrepreneurs all across America:

> *I came back to Yorktown, and it turned out this is the place I was looking for those 30 years, this little gem of a place that's really beautiful where I know everybody. I can open the windows and the breeze flows through. I got views of the river out of two windows. I ride that scooter out there a mile across the battlefield and take a nap during lunch. The sense of community in a small town is the appeal. In a mile drive on my scooter, I will average five waves. It is just that I know everybody. It is definitely a lifestyle choice. Most people go into something like this thinking, 'I can make money.' I went into it thinking, 'OK, I want to make jewelry, so what can I do to make money making jewelry?'*

The other 99 entrepreneurs we interviewed were just as captivating and inspiring as Hank. As we left each interview, I said to my teammates, "I love this job." They got tired of hearing it—*we know, we know, you love this job*—but they love it, too. The heroic entrepreneurs we discovered are part of an army of 28 million small-business owners across America. According to the Small Business Administration (SBA), 55 percent of American workers are employed at smaller companies rather than large corporations. And yet the behemoths get all the media attention. Thousands of articles have been written about Apple, Microsoft, Facebook, Amazon, Google, and eBay. Very few are ever written about companies like Viccellio Goldsmith & Fine Jewelry. Yet millions of entrepreneurs are building fascinating businesses under the media's radar. We seldom learn specific details about these everyday American heroes. But having just met 100 of them, I can say with certainty that they have a lot to teach us about building successful companies.

Main Street vs. Wall Street

During my career as an entrepreneur, business consultant, and director of two centers for entrepreneurship, I have watched how the strategies for teaching new venturing have evolved. The prevailing attitude today is that big businesses are superior to small ones, that companies that can scale quickly are better than those that can't, and that lifestyle businesses are not always worth building. I have heard many academic pundits ask, "Why would you start your own company if all you are doing is creating a job for yourself?" Consequently, the dominant doctrine for teaching entrepreneurship is what I call the Silicon Valley model. It goes like this: You create a prototype that you can test quickly, preferably in the tech industry. You find a group of users and gain proof of concept. You raise capital and scale the business as rapidly as possible. You plan an exit strategy. And you shoot for a 10x return to investors. The ultimate coup of the Silicon Valley model is to go public and sell your shares on Wall Street. This provides tremendous liquidity for you and your investors. The funny thing about this strategy is that less than 1 percent of new startups ever receive venture funding, and only 10 percent of *those* companies ever go public.

None of the entrepreneurs we interviewed used the Silicon Valley strategy. Instead, they implemented what I call the Main Street model: They found a desirable location where they wanted to live, they found a need in the community that they were uniquely qualified to fill, they used a host of resources other than money to get started, they diversified their products based on intimate interaction with their customers, they were driven by purpose and passion, and they became vital contributors to their communities. Most receive no funding at all, and very few have an exit strategy. Since they are merging livelihood and lifestyle to build their dream, they don't *want* to bail out. Allen Lim, founder of Skratch

Labs, summarized this attitude best when he told us his exit strategy was "Probably dying."

I have no problem with the Silicon Valley model of entrepreneurship; it leads to remarkable innovations and the creation of thousands of jobs. However, teaching it as the primary strategy for launching companies is like telling aspiring entrepreneurs they can all become the president of the United States or play in the NBA. Very few people can found a $100 million tech company or go public on Wall Street, but just about anyone can do what the small-town entrepreneurs we met all across America are doing. The Main Street model is more about the intangibles: purpose, passion, perseverance, teamwork, exceptional service, creating value, pivoting to opportunities, and giving back to the community. To the chagrin of the "big is better" evangelists, most of the small-business owners I have consulted with during the past 20 years would much rather operate their own company than work for a large corporation, even though they may have only created a job for themselves. You will see how the entrepreneurs in this book have intentionally chosen Main Street over Wall Street. The Main Street model they follow works for everyone; the Wall Street strategy works for an infinitesimal few.

The TransAmerica Trail

To study companies on Wall Street you read annual reports, fly across the country on jets, and visit corporate headquarters in big cities. You meet with executives in suits who have MBAs and listen to their rehearsed presentations. If you travel by car, you drive on freeways, stop at chain gas stations, eat at chain restaurants, and sleep at chain hotels. I have done this many times during my career.

Studying companies on Main Street requires a different mode of travel altogether. You need to see the terrain, the communities, the schools, the post offices, and the people firsthand. You need to meet the entrepreneurs in their own environment to see how they have successfully merged livelihood and lifestyle. Traveling by bike is a unique research methodology that matches the subject of study. It allows for a much more scenic and sensory-rich experience than traveling by plane or car; it is the perfect way for a team of entrepreneurial anthropologists to study a unique and important segment of our culture up close.

Several years ago I discovered the TransAmerica Trail, a dedicated bicycle route across the country. It begins on the beach in Oregon and ends on the beach in Virginia. It was created in 1976 to commemorate the bicentennial of the Declaration of Independence. It was purposely designed to avoid large cities, and it features some of our most beautiful scenery. It crosses 10 states through the heart of America—Oregon, Idaho, Montana, Wyoming, Colorado, Kansas, Missouri, Illinois, Kentucky, and Virginia—and passes through more than 100 small towns. In 1976, a group of more than 2,000 cyclists completed this journey to celebrate our tremendous freedoms as a country, and to experience the neighborhoods and communities of Main Street America. It seemed to me like a splendid way to study successful small-town entrepreneurs.

The problem was I wasn't sure I could complete the journey by bike, and I wasn't sure I could ever find the time to do it. Then a couple of summers ago, an amazing thing happened; I had a week of white space on my calendar, something that almost never happens to an entrepreneur, consultant, and professor. It was also the week of my wedding anniversary, and my wife, Mary, and I wanted to do something exhilarating. I decided to take the advice I am always giving my entrepreneurship students: *Don't dream about being big until you have success being small.* In other words, prove your idea works before you jump in big time. So I decided to ride part of the TransAmerica Trail, from the Pacific Coast in Oregon to the Snake River in Idaho, a distance of nearly 500 miles. It was a test drive to see if I could do the bigger ride across the continent. I needed to prove I could do 500 miles before I set out to bike 4,000.

I did the biker's "wheel dip" in the Pacific Ocean in the small town of Florence, Oregon, and then headed east on Highway 126. Mary would drive our car about 100 miles ahead, find a hotel for the night, jump on her bike, and then ride back to meet me with massive amounts of food to replace the 3,000 to 4,000 calories I was burning each day. We would then ride back to the hotel together. Mary has always been a staunch supporter of my insanity. I'm not sure how I got so lucky. Before I met her, she lived in Brazil as a foreign exchange student, worked on a kibbutz in Israel, and spent time on a Greek island—all before she was 21 years old. This was the kind of life I wanted, and I fell in love with her instantly. Over the years we have endorsed each other's multiple schemes. This time, she was my support crew extraordinaire.

Oregon is a gorgeous, bike-friendly state. We rode along coastal waterways, forests, magical volcano fields, mountains, canyons, lakes, and rivers. The wildlife was spectacular. One day a bear came out of the forest and stood on his hind legs as though applauding while Mary rode by. Equally interesting were the small cities and businesses we visited along the way. While there were some ramshackle ghost towns, there were plenty of small, vibrant communities as well. For example, Sisters has grown from 929 to 2,118 residents since the year 2000, a gain of 113 percent. And Redmond has grown from 13,481 to 26,924 residents during the same time period, a gain of 94 percent. The people in these small towns were friendly and industrious, running interesting businesses, providing superb service, and living the good life.

When I crossed the Idaho border and jumped into the Snake River, I had proved the ride was doable. I committed to the cross-country trip the following summer, even though I still had a number of unanswered questions: Could I do the full distance without accident or injury? How much would a journey like this cost? Would successful entrepreneurs be willing to share their stories and secrets to success? Despite these concerns, I made a solemn pledge to do whatever it took to make this venture happen. I would use human power to study remarkable entrepreneurs who could shed light on a new career path for our changing economy. Figure 1–1 on page 8 shows the TransAmerica Trail I selected for the journey.

Our Courageous Crew

I was accompanied on this adventure by the greatest team ever: my wife, Mary; my business partner, Shawn; and my son and videographer, Jay. Mary was training for the Ironman Arizona during our trip, so she biked every other day and then ran up to 14 miles and swam in

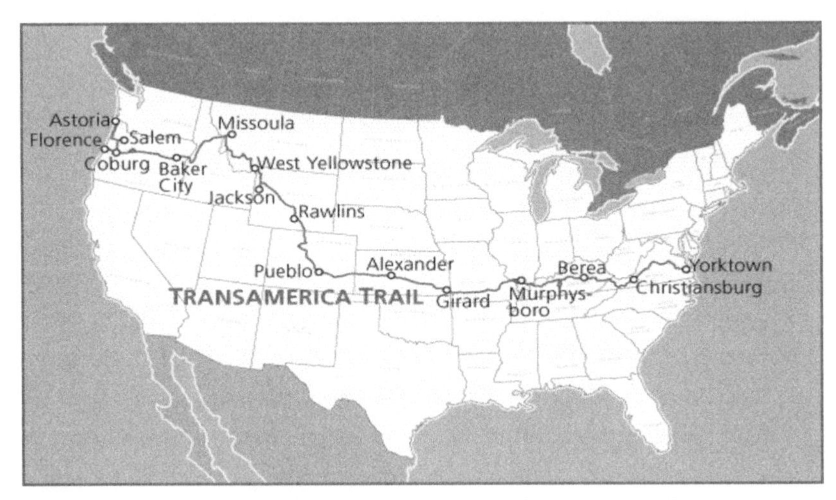

Figure 1–1: **The TransAmerica Trail**

rivers, lakes, and pools on the odd days—as if biking several thousand miles was not enough. She was by far the strongest athlete on the tour. Shawn thought she was out of her mind, but since I have lived with her for 35 years, I knew it was just standard procedure. On the days Mary and I rode together, we would experience what I affectionately called "Mary's Madness." It was something deep in her core that not even she understood, but it went like this: about 40 to 50 miles into the ride, she would start hammering the pedals. She always claimed she didn't know it was happening, but she would pass me with a look of total concentration on her face and leave me in her jet stream. When I finally caught up with her five or ten miles later, we would have this conversation:

"Mary, why are we going 28 miles an hour?"
"We're not going that fast."
"Look at your computer."
"I'm just doing what feels good."
"Yeah, but I have to ride another 100 miles tomorrow."
"OK, so what do you want to do?"
"*Slow down!*"

After returning from our cross-country excursion, Mary took second place in her age division at the Ironman Arizona, with a time of 12 hours and 19 minutes. After swimming 2.4 miles, she had an amazing bike ride, covering the 112-mile course in just over six hours. She missed qualifying for the world championships in Kona, Hawaii, by one place. Of course, I was immensely proud of her.

Shawn is the cofounder of our online training company, My New Enterprise. He and I have done a number of consulting projects together during the past few years. Shawn is tall, handsome, smart, and exceptionally articulate. He can explain the findings of my research better than I can. He is a bit quirky at times, but hey, we all are, especially when cooped up in a motorhome for eight weeks. Shawn handled the three of us remarkably well. He was our navigator during the trip, worked closely with our sponsors, and interviewed some of our entrepreneurs.

Jay is our videographer and chief creative officer at My New Enterprise. He is also my incredibly gifted son, but of course I'm not biased. Jay is a talented musician with a great deal of experience in performing and merchandising products. He is also an excellent documentary filmmaker and a whiz at anything technical. Jay was our workhorse during the tour. He would ride during the day, film all the entrepreneurs, and edit video late into the night. He by far did the most work during our wild ride across America.

In order to complete this adventure, I followed a rigorous training schedule. I built to a base of 100 miles every week, and then added 50 miles per week each month. I eventually went from 100 to 250 miles a week, which I maintained for the last four months prior to our departure. I committed to ride the entire 4,000 miles. Shawn, Mary, and Jay would then rotate in across the country, so there would usually be three of us riding each day. The person not riding would drive the bus, confirm appointments, go shopping, and wrangle for the riders. This plan worked great unless it hailed or snowed, when I couldn't get anyone to ride with me. I suffered alone.

Finding the Entrepreneurs

Approximately half of the towns on the TransAmerica Trail have fewer than 1,000 residents. The other half have populations between

1,000 and 30,000 people. Only five of the cities we visited have more than 30,000 residents: Eugene, Oregon; Missoula, Montana; Boulder, Colorado; Pueblo, Colorado; and Charlottesville, Virginia. Most of the towns with populations of 1,000 or more have remained stable or grown during the past decade; half of these cities have experienced double-digit growth, greater than that of the country during the same time period. So these are attractive expanding communities.

With this background information, we followed three broad criteria in our search for entrepreneurial role models: 1) we focused on towns with at least 1,000 residents; 2) we looked for towns with a growing population; and 3) we concentrated on entrepreneurs who have been in business for at least five years, which is the time it takes for a company to stabilize and prove sustainability. Though we generally followed these rules, we collected intriguing stories along the way wherever we found them. So you will also meet some thriving business builders in rural towns of a few hundred people.

To find these entrepreneurs, we searched city websites, contacted the local chambers of commerce, read newspaper articles, reviewed business publications, studied company websites, and asked a lot of people, "Who are the best entrepreneurs in your town?" We started with a large list and eventually whittled it down. Our final cast of characters—working in a wide variety of businesses in all kinds of industries—reflects the great diversity of small-town America. Their stories that follow are taken directly from interview transcripts and follow-up phone calls. All quotes are presented as they were spoken with only minor editing to eliminate redundancy and improve clarity. Thus, you will experience the passion and insights from these role models as we did in their presence. They teach us a great deal about finding an attractive place to live, starting the right ventures, overcoming adversity, thriving in a fishbowl environment, dazzling communities, and living life joyfully—all important things to know in our new technology-driven economy.

REFLECTION

Personal Inventory

So here we are on the beach in Yorktown. After months of planning and a fair amount of suffering, we have finally completed our journey. Now I have a story to tell about some amazing people, the keys to entrepreneurial success, and time-proven principles for merging livelihood and lifestyle. It is a story of passion, tenacity, and working hard for the American Dream. I will share this story with you against the backdrop of our bizarre and beautiful escapade across the country. You will see that the road is not always easy, and often pretty rough. And just as we encountered on our journey, all these entrepreneurs experience zeal and fear, surge and retreat, exhilaration and exhaustion, laughter and tears, and ultimate triumph. Their collective stories, and the keys to success they teach us, comprise a career handbook for the 21st century.

So let's go back to Oregon and start pedaling. I promise you won't be disappointed if you come along. In fact, I think you will enjoy the ride as much as I did—maybe more, because you won't have to sit on a bike seat for 4,000 miles, suffer through rain and snow, climb dozens of humongous mountains, or be cooped up in a motorhome every night with three other people. Who knows—you may decide the challenge sounds alluring and decide to take the journey yourself someday. It was so extraordinary I would not hesitate to do it again. So let's start this trip across the heartland together. Here are some questions to ponder as you continue reading.

1. Is your current job vulnerable to displacement due to technology development?
2. Are you satisfied with the place you are currently living?
3. How do you personally view small businesses versus large corporations?
4. Do you have several business ideas you are thinking about pursuing?
5. Are you ready to create your own company and achieve your dreams?

CHAPTER

2

Start with a Clear Purpose

"What I know for sure: There is no greater gift you can give or receive than to honor your calling. It's why you were born. And how you become most truly alive."

—Oprah Winfrey, media mogul, entrepreneur, philanthropist

The weatherman on the local news channel said there would be 30-mile-per-hour winds blowing down the coast in the morning. *Great!* We were sitting in our hotel room at the Driftwood Shores on the beach in Florence, Oregon. The following morning we would start our daunting 4,000-mile bike ride across America. Do you know what 30 mph winds do to you on a bike? It's not pretty. Oh well, we knew it was going to be tough—we might as well start off with a bang.

In the morning, after eating what became our standard breakfast of granola, yogurt, bananas, and lots of chocolate milk, we unloaded our bikes off the back of the motorhome and headed to the beach. After clearing the building, the wind caught our deep rim wheels and nearly blew us over. What should we do? If we let go of our bikes, the wind would blow them to Mexico. If we hung on, we'd all end up south of the border. We turned our bikes sideways with the wind and soldiered on. When we reached the water, we dipped our wheels in the surf, let out a rather nervous and anemic cheer, and trudged back to the parking lot to start our ride. *What were we thinking?*

No matter what, we were totally committed to this escapade. We had been declaring our intentions publicly for months. We had thrown a kickoff event at Utah State University, where I direct the Clark Center for Entrepreneurship. We served lunch to hundreds of students and faculty members and made our bold claims: "We are taking a proactive stand against the coming employment crisis. We will introduce a new career model that will help people create jobs. We are reinventing the American Dream." We had raised $28,455 on Kickstarter, and several articles appeared about our tour in newspapers and magazines, including one in *Inc.* titled "This Sweaty Professor Wants to Interview You About Your Company." And two days before our departure we held a farewell party at my home where we answered all questions in the affirmative: *Yeah, we are really doing this. We are not quitting, no matter what. We can handle the big mountains. Of course we will ride in the rain.* The beauty of making public commitments is that there is no turning back. We had no choice but to succeed. We had crossed the Rubicon.

So D-Day had finally arrived. Mary and I saddled up our carbon-fiber steeds and started down the coast. The strong wind at our backs gave us a sweet blow down Rhododendron Street, but then we turned east. We were blown all over the highway for the next hour, but once we dropped behind the hills, the wind quieted down. It was an interesting first hour of the 245 more that would follow.

As it turned out, the winds in Oregon that day proved to be a minor challenge compared to those that would follow. We faced rain, hail, and snow in Montana; near frostbite at 7,000 feet in Wyoming; daylong headwinds in Kansas; countless steep hills we had to climb in the Ozarks; a crash in Hazard, Kentucky; and torrential rains across Virginia. But our purpose pulled us through all these trials with hope, optimism, and enthusiasm. We were on a mission, not to be deterred. We were meeting and interviewing some of the most interesting entrepreneurs on the planet and sharing their stories with the world. We were 100 percent committed to helping people create their own jobs and build successful companies. This drove us relentlessly and impacted all our thinking and behavior. We met other riders along the way who were riding across America just to say they had done it. Some of them were wondering if the bragging rights were worth it. One guy said he was going to throw his bike in the ocean when he got to Virginia and never ride it again. That's how much fun he was having. We never felt that way during our journey because we were doing something much bigger than simply riding our bikes across America. We had a very clear and powerful purpose.

Our Mission-Driven Entrepreneurs

This same resilient sense of mission was one of the first things we noticed about the entrepreneurs we interviewed. They are driven by a purpose much bigger than themselves. While they all realize they need to make money, none of them mentioned that as a primary driver. Instead, they want to change the world in their own small or large way, create jobs in their beloved hometowns, and give back to their communities. They are solving a problem that intrigues them and doing something they are passionate about, while providing the best service in their industry.

This strong sense of purpose is a critical launching pad for a new venture. It does four things for your growing business: 1) it gets you through the difficult times you will inevitably face, 2) it sets a higher standard of excellence for your business, 3) it appeals to like-minded team members who share your values, and 4) it attracts and keeps customers who love what you are doing. We will discuss these four benefits of having a strong sense of purpose later in the chapter. For now, let me introduce you to eight of the mission-driven entrepreneurs who represent our larger group. Notice how their strong "why" for building their business impacts everything they do.

Benny and Julie Benson

Benny and Julie grew up on farms in Colorado with horses, livestock, and wide-open spaces. When Benny was in high school, he traded a horse for his first motorcycle. The second motorcycle he bought was in two buckets full of parts. Then he started building and selling motorcycles, cars, and boats. He and Julie both earned degrees in mechanical engineering and moved to California to work in corporate America. Of his first day on the job, Benny says, "I wanted to get there early on the first day, so I left two hours early; I showed up 15 minutes late. That was my introduction to traffic in Southern California."

Benny and Julie enjoyed working on various engineering projects. In particular, they loved creating renewable energy from waste fuels; they just didn't love doing it in Los Angeles. As Julie explains:

> *When our daughter was starting school, we took a look around at our environment and our lifestyle, and we didn't like what we were seeing in Southern California. It was the rat race down there, and the rats were winning. So we thought, 'We've got to get out of here.' We just wanted a simpler life.*

So they started looking for a new place to live. Ten days after discovering Sisters, Oregon, they moved there to enjoy a better life for their family. Benny describes the criteria they used in making this decision:

> *Quality of life became the driver. It wasn't 'What [are we] going to do?' It was 'Where are we going to end up?' We had to have a major ski area within an hour, we had to have an Olympic-size pool within an hour, and we had to be able to stand out on our deck naked and not worry about somebody looking. Not that I really cared in California, but Julie might have a different perspective [laughs].*

Initially, they started designing bio-gas plants that use waste fuels produced at landfills, wastewater treatment facilities, and manure storage sites. They operated their business out of a bedroom and flew to various job sites from the airport in Sisters. After designing a number of plants, they felt they were in a strong position to start building them as well, so they did. Next they developed an IT solution so they could operate these plants remotely. Now they offer a complete one-stop service to their customers, including designing, building, and managing renewable energy plants—all from their headquarters in Sisters. Eight years after starting Energyneering Solutions, they have 60 employees and have designed and built more than 50 renewable energy plants that are producing power for 150,000 households. Of their new life, Julie says:

> *I really like engineering. It isn't about what we do for money, it's about what we can offer the world because engineering to me is really just problem solving. It's identifying an issue and hoping to make it better somehow. . . . Now we live on a property where we have donkeys and horses and sheep and dogs and cats and birds. We are heavily involved in showing horses, which is not something we could have done in Southern California.*

Benny agrees they have achieved their purpose of merging livelihood and lifestyle in their new location. As we are leaving the interview, he says, "We can all take a half day or a day. If it's snowing, we're skiing. We shouldn't really be here today, we should be on the lake right now, but you guys were coming [laughs]."

Hugh and Skeeter Reed

Hugh and Skeeter are also living the lifestyle of their dreams. They own the historic Oregon Hotel in Mitchell, Oregon, a town of 130 people. Hugh is built like a large wedge, with broad shoulders, big arms, and narrow hips. When I interviewed him, he was wearing a sleeveless T-shirt, and I noticed that his upper arms were nearly as large as my thighs. His upper body strength has come from genetics and years of hard physical work. Though Hugh is nearly 80 years old, you don't want to mess with him. Over the past 16 years, he has enjoyed wrestling with his black bear, Henry. He acquired Henry from the local sheriff's brother, who was moving out of the area. When Henry was a year old and weighed 400 pounds, he and Hugh duked it out to determine who was going to be the alpha male in the relationship:

One day he bit me, and it pissed me off. I thought to myself, well, you son of a gun, bite the hand that feeds you. Anyone in their right mind would have got out of the pen, but we got into a real battle. I had to win or get ate, so I won. I found a trick with a canine where you get them by the top nose, put your thumb right between their fangs, and they go down like they'd been shot. Henry and I had an understanding after that; he's my buddy.

For years, Hugh was called the "Tree Man" because he slept in a tree on his property. In 1972 he bought 80 acres outside Mitchell. Originally, it was just a camp with no house, electricity, or running water. He brought chickens, goats, and horses with him. The animals bothered him at night, so he built a bed in a tree. Even so, one of the chickens climbed up the tree, slept with him at night, and became his pet.

To make a living over the years, Hugh has been a rancher, horse trainer, gas station owner, restaurant owner, and construction worker. He met Skeeter on one of his jobs. Her given name is Waunita, but her family has called her Skeeter for years. "I buzz around and bother people," she says. When Hugh first saw her, he says, he knew she was going to be trouble, and she was—they ended up getting married. Their powerful purpose for buying and remodeling the old Oregon Hotel is to provide an income for Skeeter for the rest of her life. Hugh is 21 years older than her, and he is committed to making sure she has a secure future. "When I die," he says, "she will always have an income; she is taken care of."

Skeeter loves life in Mitchell—the people, their ranch, their hotel, and their guests. She is passionate about making their quaint and rustic inn attractive to people passing through the area: "It's not like the Hilton; it's like going back in time," she says. "People that stay here say it's like going to Grandma's house. You hear creaks in the floor and you think it's a ghost. I personally have never seen a ghost, but who knows?"

Gail and Will Williams

Gail and Will live on a stunning ranch outside White Bird, Idaho. If you have ever ridden on a ski lift, you have probably sat on a padded cushion made by their company, Idaho Sewing for Sports. Gail and Will discovered northern Idaho on a family vacation. They were overwhelmed with the beauty of the area and decided they wanted to raise their kids there. They started their business in a chicken coop with $2,000 and a dilapidated old truck. Gail was a seamstress and had been sewing seat covers for truckers in California. In an effort to earn income in their new home, she packed up her three young boys and drove through a blinding snowstorm to the Sun Valley Ski Resort. She persuaded them to let her re-cover the padding around their lift towers. On her way home, the knob fell off the stick shift, so she drove 25 miles in second gear. From that beginning, Gail went out selling to ski resorts all over the United States. Today, Idaho Sewing for Sports employs 20 people and makes padded cushions for hundreds of ski resorts around the world—all from a gorgeous ridge in northern Idaho.

While their initial purpose was to live in a spectacular location, Gail, Will, and their son Gunther now run the business to bless the lives of people who need jobs. Gail tells the story of a man with one arm who came to them looking for work. She wanted to help him but didn't think he could operate the equipment they use to cut and sew their products. She gave him a chance and says he was phenomenal! He later told Gail he was ready to commit suicide because no one would give him a chance and he couldn't take care of his family. After he worked at Idaho Sewing for Sports, other doors opened for him in his career.

On another occasion, a woman who had worked on Wall Street and run a computer company in Boise approached Gail about a job. Her career had been very stressful, and she had just experienced a nasty divorce. She had two boys, was very depressed, and was looking for a place to heal. Gail explains:

> *She came out to answer our ad for a seamstress. I mean, she's suit and briefcase and I'm thinking, 'Why would you want to work up here in the mountains?' She said, 'I just need to get away from all of it for a while.' So I told her, 'I am big with family, and mothers should be mothers. So you can come to work, and your boys can come, too. They can work till noon and then hit the river and play.' So they did that all that summer.*

Gail has also allowed women in town to work for her in their own homes. One was a grandmother who was raising her four grandchildren. Gail set up a table and sewing machine in the woman's home and carried supplies back and forth because the woman didn't have a driver's license. She was able to care for her grandchildren until they were grown, and she continued to work for the company until she died. Here is how Gail's son Gunther, who is now the CEO of the company, explains their unique philosophy:

> *The purpose of this business is to serve the employees that work here. I mean, that's the only reason to have employees in my standpoint. If it is good for the employees, it is good for us. It's not about the company or the money. . . . In my experience, the more I concentrate on what I need, the harder it is to attain. If I can get beyond that and focus on the people that I serve, the bottom line takes care of itself.*

Jason Kintzler

Jason is the founder of the game-changing company Pitchengine. He grew up near the spectacular Wind River Mountains in Lander, Wyoming. Over the years he noticed how people would go away to acquire their wealth or "mine their money" and then come back to the place they really wanted to live. So during his early career as a news anchor and public relations consultant, he started asking himself, *What if I could do what I am passionate about in the place I want to live forever?* His answer led him back to Lander—home of 7,000 cowboys, ranchers, rock climbers, mountain bikers, and other fascinating characters. It's an unlikely place to create a disruptive technology that would transform the public relations industry.

What Jason created was a robust content creation platform to help corporations authentically tell their story and build their brand through social media. He marketed his service with an unparalleled work ethic: attending conferences, displaying at trade shows, speaking at universities, aggressively blogging, and working with public relations firms. Two years after inception, Jason was offered $9 million for his business, which he turned down to continue his quest of merging livelihood and lifestyle on Main Street, USA. Today, his content creation platform, Pitchengine, is used by more than 50,000 companies worldwide, including Walmart, PepsiCo, Geico, and Budweiser. Jason describes the advantages he sees in building his business in Lander:

> *I don't think people realize the potential of having companies like this in a small town. If you have FedEx or UPS, and you have an airport, you can do it anywhere. What I love is that we are able to help revitalize Main Street. Being part of the fiber of the community is a really big deal. Other businesses that already exist start to capitalize on the momentum. And being an underdog from a small town helps us to be more creative and scrappy. I don't want to go away, so our decisions matter, and that's exciting to me. Having the right people around, doing things for the right reasons, fires me up. If things blow up and we make $20 million tomorrow, I don't think it is going to change me much. I might have a new tractor and a bigger plot, but I'm not going to be jet-setting or anything like that.*

Jean and Barry Anderson

One of the most interesting visits we made during our cross-country tour was to Sundance Sheepskin & Leather in the mountains above Guffey, Colorado. The morning of our visit, we had a spectacular bike ride from Silverthorne to Breckenridge, up Hoosier Pass to 11,542 feet elevation, and then down to the tiny hamlet of Guffey, population 98. Barry and Jean Anderson started Sundance Sheepskin & Leather on a 40-acre parcel of land they purchased in 1971. To get to their business, you turn off Highway 9 onto a gravel road at mile marker 23. Then you drive a mile and a half to an intersection of dirt roads and take a map out of a red coffee can hanging from Barry and Jean's mailbox. This treasure map leads you four miles up the mountain to their home and workshop, located at 9,300 feet elevation. It was so steep at the end of the road that Mary had the pedal to the floor on our motorhome, but we were only going five miles an hour. The big Ford V10 engine was groaning so loudly I thought it was going to explode. Mary thought it was so frightening that when we left she refused to drive down the mountain and got out and walked.

Barry and Jean bought their land for $350 down and $82 a month for 10 years. As Jean explains, "We wanted to find a place we could homestead and do whatever we wanted; this property was so cheap we couldn't afford not to buy it." Knowing they had to make a living, they acquired a truckload of sheepskins from a friend. Barry and Jean had both learned to sew from their mothers, and Jean had experience working in her family's business. They started making vests, moccasins, hats, mittens, and other products from sheepskin. Initially, they sold custom-made clothing for people who visited the small storefront they rented in Canyon City, about 30 miles away. Later they started making standard products they sold through arts and crafts shows around the country. When their daughter finished her degree in engineering, she returned to the family business and developed their online presence. Their son also returned to the business after earning degrees in both electrical and mechanical engineering. He bought 40 acres next to his parents and assists with manufacturing, distribution, and anything else that needs to be done.

Today, Sundance Sheepskin & Leather sells products through three primary channels: ecommerce, arts and crafts shows, and a retail store run by their daughter in Buena Vista, Colorado. Their bread and butter product is their "Colorado Moccasin," which they make in a wide variety of sizes and colors. The UPS truck makes the trek up their dirt road most days to pick up orders that are delivered all over the United States. Although their business has grown significantly over the years, it has never been primarily about making money. It's about living in a beautiful location, working together as a family, and making fabulous niche products that people absolutely love. As Barry concludes, "I like making things, and I like making things for people. The reward I get is from the person who says, 'I really like what you do.'" Sundance Sheepskin & Leather has made a remarkable lifestyle possible for the Anderson family.

Debbie and Mike Brooks

The purpose of Spinach Can Collectibles is to further the spirit of Popeye, the cartoon sailor, in Chester, Illinois. For decades, Chester was known as the home of the Menard Correctional Center, the maximum-security prison that houses Illinois' most notorious criminals. In a town of 8,586 people, approximately 900 work at the prison, which houses almost 3,700 inmates. John Wayne Gacy, the monster who murdered 33 boys and young men, was housed there until his execution. Robert Ben Rhoades, the truck driver suspected of raping and murdering at least 50 women, is still there, sentenced to life without parole. What city wants to be known as home to these guys?

Debbie and Mike wanted to "put Chester on the map for something more positive than the prison." They are both die-hard Popeye fans. When Debbie was a young girl, she found strength during a serious crisis by thinking about Popeye, and she has loved him ever since. Mike has also loved Popeye for as long as he can remember. After they got married, they started collecting Popeye memorabilia and launched the Popeye Fan Club. They visited Chester in 1990 when they learned it was the hometown of Popeye's creator, Elzie Segar. They were shocked to only find one statue of their beloved hero in the town. They moved to Chester in 1994 to help change the situation—their driving purpose.

Mike and Debbie opened Spinach Can Collectibles in the old opera house where Segar worked as a projectionist. Three of Segar's main characters are based on actual residents of Chester. Popeye's model was Frank "Rocky" Fiegel, a local tough guy who was good with his fists; Olive Oyl was based on Dora Paskel, the proprietor of the general store; and J. Wellington Wimpy was modeled after Segar's boss at the opera house, J. William Schuchert. Spinach Can Collectibles is part museum and part store. The museum tells the story of Popeye, and the store sells memorabilia: shirts, hats, buttons, books, games, corncob pipes, and even spinach.

Popeye is now better known in Chester than the prison, as people from all 50 states and more than 70 countries have come to visit his hometown. The annual Popeye Picnic, where a new statue of one of Segar's characters is unveiled each year, is attended by thousands of visitors. The town now has 11 statues of Popeye and his cohorts and plans to add five more by 2020. The Boy Scouts, policemen, and firemen wear Popeye patches on their uniforms. While Mike and Debbie Brooks are only part of the movement to transform this city, they represent what passionate entrepreneurs can accomplish when they have a burning purpose to do something that benefits the broader community.

Shari McCallister

Shari McCallister was born and raised in Houston, Missouri, an amiable town of 2,117 people, and has lived there her whole life. She was laid off from a factory job in 1990 when she was just 20 years old. While she was visiting the local flower shop, the owner said, "Why don't you buy my store, since you are out of work?" Shari went home and talked with her parents about the idea, and they were supportive. She was able to acquire a small loan from a friend, and two weeks later was the proud owner of D & L Florist. Shari was inspired by the song "I'm Gonna Be Somebody" by Travis Tritt—she decided she was going to be somebody in the floral industry. She read a lot of magazines and took classes in Springfield, Missouri. She also received great mentoring from the local funeral director and an interior designer in town. The business continued to grow, and in 1995, she secured a bank loan for a remodel and an addition to the store. Shari just celebrated her 25th anniversary in business.

When we asked Shari how she had thrived for so many years, she told us this story. A few weeks earlier, a man had brought his young son, Levi, into the store. Levi's sister, McKenzie, and their grandmother had just been killed in a car accident. The man was divorced, and the grandmother was his ex-wife's mother. Levi was heartbroken. Shari blew up some pink balloons and took out a marker. She wrote, "I love you, from Levi" on one of the balloons, went outside, and sent them to McKenzie in heaven. Shari had just received a warm and unexpected thank-you card from the family. What she loves most is contributing to the happiest and saddest experiences of people in her hometown. She explains: "It is little things like this that keep me going. I feel that God has put me here for a reason. That's what keeps me motivated."

Aaron Taylor

One of the most inspiring entrepreneurs we met, who exudes the power of purpose, was a teenager named Aaron Taylor. We were at a lively auction in Damascus, Virginia, on a Saturday night—it was definitely the place to be. The auctioneer was roaring at 90 miles an hour, selling anything and everything people brought to the party. Outside the auction house was a food cart owned by Aaron. He called it Aaron's Place. A few years earlier, Aaron's mother had been diagnosed with Susac's syndrome; there are only about 100 known cases of this disease in the world. It is an autoimmune disorder that blocks the smallest blood vessels in the brain, retinas, and inner ear. Symptoms include intense migraines, frequent vomiting, hearing loss, slurred speech, confusion, depression, anxiety, and changes in personality.

As the medical bills mounted, Aaron's father sought help from family members, churches, government agencies, and nonprofit organizations. Little assistance was available. As the costs continued to rise, the family went from a middle-class lifestyle to near poverty. Aaron wasn't willing to sit around and let this happen; he wanted to help. He found a mentor who taught him all about the concession business, acquired a table and cooking equipment, and started working at fairs and events. After a year, he bought his food cart. When we met him, he had two licenses to do business in Virginia. One allowed him to operate his cart on the streets in the nearby town of Abingdon. The other allowed him to work at fairs and events statewide, which he did on weekends.

Aaron ran his business for two years, from the time he was 17 to 19 years old. His father told me, "For Aaron to stick around and help his parents was a godsend. I can't tell you how much his business helped our family." Since our visit with the Taylors, they learned that people with Susac's syndrome do better in warmer climates at lower elevations, so they moved to the coast of North Carolina. Aaron wants to continue operating his business there until his mother's illness is resolved and the bills are paid. Regardless of what he decides to do, Aaron teaches us a valuable lesson: there is always something we can do to solve a problem, create value for others, and earn a living for ourselves. If there is a strong purpose behind our efforts, we can always make something happen. Working to help his mom was Aaron's motivation to launch his business and keep it running.

The Power of Purpose

The power of purpose is a huge key to building a successful business. The eight entrepreneurs you just met, and all the others we interviewed, can clearly articulate *why* they are doing what they are doing. As mentioned earlier, having a clear and motivating purpose gets you through the challenging times you will face, sets a higher standard of excellence for your business, entices team members to join you in your cause, and attracts and keeps customers who love what you are doing. Let's discuss each of these benefits in more detail.

Purpose Provides Staying Power

I think the best book ever written on the power of purpose is *Man's Search for Meaning* by Viktor Frankl. Prior to World War II, Frankl was a neurologist and psychiatrist in private practice in Vienna. In 1942, he and his family were sent to various concentration camps by the Nazis—including the notorious Auschwitz and Dachau. Frankl was the only one to survive; the rest of his family, including his wife, died in the camps.

During his time in the camps, being a psychiatrist, he was extremely interested in the human dynamics he saw there, particularly in who lived and who died. Frankl observed that it was not the physically biggest or strongest who survived, but those who found some kind of meaning in their suffering. In other words, those who found purpose in their lives, even in the midst of misery, continued to live. Those who lost all purpose in their lives died.

Frankl also noticed that the highest number of deaths in the camp occurred in January. Mentally, these unfortunate prisoners had decided they could not bear another year in the camp and had counted on being released before the end of the year. When the New Year came and went and they were still imprisoned, they gave up and died. Hence, Frankl's now-famous words: "Life is never made unbearable by circumstances, but only by lack of meaning and purpose . . . He who has a WHY to live, can bear with almost any HOW."

This same principle is critical in building a successful enterprise. My observation over the years is that most businesses take longer, cost more, and earn less than you think, at least in the short run, and there are lots of bumps and bruises along the way. If you are only doing it for the money, it is too easy to bail out when the road gets rocky. However, if you really believe in what you are doing, it is much easier to find the strength to first survive and then thrive. You will enjoy the journey more and believe it will all be worth it in the end. In fact, I don't think you can build a successful business in the long run if you don't have a higher purpose than financial gain. The entrepreneurs you met above, and the others we interviewed, are not just enduring well, they are enjoying the ride, because they have a strong and motivating purpose driving their work—just like our purpose fueled our bike ride across America.

Purpose Encourages Excellence

If you have a clear purpose for your business and are in it for the long haul, you do things differently from those who want to get in and out quickly. As I mentioned earlier, none of the entrepreneurs we interviewed have a clear exit strategy, and most have no intention of exiting at all. They are doing something they really believe in, and in the process, they're building the lifestyle of their dreams. So why would they want to exit?

When your driving purpose is strong, everything you do is consistent with that. The things you do are important now, and your fulfillment happens in real time. You aren't doing things to make more money in the short run so you can have a more lucrative exit. You create great products for your customers because it's critical to your purpose. You hire and train excellent team members because it's vital to your purpose. You give phenomenal customer service because it is essential to your purpose. You offer authentic service to your community because it is integral to your purpose. These practices are not means to an end; they are ends in and of themselves. This consistency of purpose leads to higher standards of excellence, superior processes, and better results in the long run.

Purpose Entices Team Members

If you have an engaging purpose and can communicate it clearly, it will help you attract a supporting cast around your business. Your supporting crew may include mentors, advisors, team members, and strategic partners. When people love what you are doing and can express their own values by working with you, they are much more likely to join your cause. These are people who can help you effectively grow your enterprise.

Having an exciting purpose beyond making money is particularly attractive to the new Millennial generation. Millennials are those born between 1982 and 2000; this group includes 83 million people and makes up 26 percent of the U.S. population. It is the largest generational group in the history of our country. Tons of research has been done on Millennials, and one finding continues to surface. Millennials are a value-driven generation: They care about the values of the companies they buy from, they care about the values of the companies they work for, and they want to participate in meaningful work in their careers.

I teach Millennials at my university, and we talk about their career aspirations every semester. Most tell me they would rather work for a company with an exciting purpose than a stodgy old business without a compelling mission—even if it means a lower salary. Since Millennials will make up the majority of the workforce in coming years, having a clear and engaging purpose will become even more critical to building successful teams.

Purpose Attracts and Keeps Customers

Dale Aramaki owns the Phillips 66 gas station in my neighborhood. He's an excellent mechanic, gives superior service, offers great prices, hires kids from the neighborhood, and participates in community activities. Dale is my car guy. When I need gas, I go to Dale. When I need inspections, I go to Dale. When I need repairs, I go to Dale. I don't shop around, I don't check prices, and I don't go to other service stations. Why? Because Dale loves being in our neighborhood, has a genuine desire to meet our needs, and has become an integral part of our community.

In his excellent book *Start with Why*, Simon Sinek makes a very compelling point: People don't buy *what* you do; they buy *why* you do it. Consequently, companies that have a powerful purpose do better than companies that don't. Their customers become fiercely loyal and don't shop elsewhere. They become Apple gals ("Think different"). They become Lexus guys ("The relentless pursuit of perfection"). They become Whole Foods families ("Whole foods, whole people, whole planet"). Sinek argues that the old-fashioned "features and benefits" model is an ongoing game of manipulation. You have to constantly explain why the benefits of your product, based on its cool features, are better than the next guy's. So every product requires constant selling. On the other hand, when people are enamored with your "why" for doing business, a features and benefits analysis only occurs within your own product line: *Do I buy model A or B?*

When people understand that your purpose is to create jobs in the city, solve an ongoing problem, provide phenomenal customer service, revitalize Main Street, address a health issue, or give back to the community, they are more inclined to support your business. They become loyal fans who only buy certain products or services from you, which is far better than constantly having to sell features and benefits. People don't buy *what* you do; they buy *why* you do it.

REFLECTION

Defining Your Purpose

Having a motivating purpose is a critical foundation for building a successful company. It is not enough by itself, but it is an important starting point. The other key factors in this book are equally important and will build upon that foundation. So make sure you get your starting point down before you jump into something that doesn't create staying power for you, your team, or your customers. The questions below will help you clarify and evaluate your purpose.

1. What is your major purpose for starting your own business?
2. Is this purpose strong enough to get you through all the challenges you will face?
3. Will this purpose motivate you to strive for excellent processes and systems?
4. Will this purpose attract other like-minded and talented people to your team?
5. Will this purpose inspire customers to become loyal fans of your business?

CHAPTER

3

Build on What You Know

"I would have loved to have come up with Twitter, who wouldn't? But I don't know anything about that. So I am doing what I know how to do, and that's make clothes for people who enjoy the outdoors."

—Steve Sullivan, founder of Stio

White Bird Hill is becoming legendary in the cycling community. It is a long steep grind from White Bird, Idaho, over a mountain pass, and down to Grangeville. The road climbs 2,700 feet in 7 miles with grades of 6 to 12 percent. Truckers try to avoid White Bird Hill when possible because it is hard on their engines and brakes. But cyclists from all over the area come and ride it to test their abilities. Since Mary is the mountain goat on our team who can climb big slopes all day long, she was my partner that day.

The views up the mountain were spectacular. Off to the right we could see a beautiful valley where the Battle of White Bird Canyon was fought in 1877. It was the first battle of the Nez Perce War between the Nez Perce Indians and the U.S. Cavalry. On the morning of June 17th, 106 soldiers clashed with 70 Indians. Most of the soldiers were inexperienced and unprepared for battle. The Indians knew the terrain well and hid in the buttes above the road. They were excellent hunters and marksmen who rode well-trained Appaloosa horses. At the end of the day, 34 soldiers were dead; all 70 Indians were still alive.

After cresting the summit, we started our descent to Grangeville. At the bottom of the hill I was surprised to see our motorhome on the side of the road. Jay and Shawn should have been in Syringa, our final destination for the day. There was an orange emergency triangle on the road in front of the bus. Jay was sitting on a camp chair eating a sandwich, and Shawn was on the phone yelling at someone. We soon found out the tread had come off one of the rear tires and flipped around, hammering the bottom of the motorhome. Jay thought the bikes had fallen off the back, and Shawn thought they had hit a kitchen sink. By the time they pulled over to inspect the damage, the drive train was bent, the muffler and tailpipe were torn off, the gas tank had shifted, the wiring to the batteries was ripped off, and the greywater tank was leaking. They weren't going anywhere!

Shawn and I jumped on our bikes and rode into Grangeville to get help. The manager from Les Schwab sent a guy out to replace the damaged tire. Dale Weeks, owner of Dale's Rescue Towing, got us to the Bear Den RV Resort a few miles away. As we sat there, broken down, trying to figure out what to do next, my enthusiasm for owning this motorhome was waning. None of us had any experience with RV maintenance, parts, or repairs. We were totally out of our league. Just like the Battle of White Bird Canyon, the more experienced Indians were winning this skirmish. We had to figure out how to keep this venture alive.

Knowing Your Industry

Most of the entrepreneurs we interviewed across America had far more experience with their industries than we had with our motorhome. About one-third of them had worked in the same industry they started their business in. Another third had worked in a related industry. Most of the remaining third were regular users of the products or services and understood the pain points and opportunities from personal experience. In other words, they knew the market from the customers' point of view. They knew the products' features, the competitors, and the missing pieces. Only a small percentage of the successful entrepreneurs I have interviewed over the past 20 years have started businesses in markets they knew absolutely nothing about. And these people generally become serious students of the industry, like Shari McCallister did when she bought her flower store in Houston, Missouri. In addition, many of these entrepreneurs bring in partners who know more about the industry than they do.

You may be thinking, "I know a woman who built a really successful company, and she had no experience in the industry whatsoever." You may also be thinking, "I know this guy who had tons of industry experience, but his business failed anyway." It's a question of probabilities. The more experience you have in your industry, the more you know about the products, services, competitors, suppliers, channels of distribution, customers, and opportunities. The less you know about your industry, the more you have to learn things through trial and error, just like we did with our motorhome. And with limited experience, you often burn through your passion, tenacity, relationships, and money before you gain traction. You can only survive so many crashes on White Bird Hill before you self-destruct and become a statistic in the business failure column. Hence, the more you build on what you already know from your own experience, the greater your probability for success. Plain and simple!

Our Experienced Entrepreneurs

Some of the remarkable entrepreneurs we met across America built successful companies around their previous experiences. Steve Sullivan and Mary DeLima built companies in industries they worked in. Sam Spayd and Allen Lim built ventures in industries related to their previous work experience. And Nicole DeBoom and Sheila Kemper Dietrich built businesses in industries where they knew the problems, pain points, and opportunities from personal experience.

Knowledge of Same Industry

Steve Sullivan is the founder of Stio in Jackson Hole, Wyoming. The company makes and sells outdoor clothing that is both functional and fashionable—the kind of clothes you want to wear every day. The product line includes jackets, vests, shirts, pants, sweaters, tees, hoodies, hats, and scarves. While Stio has two retail stores, one in Jackson Hole and one in Chicago, it primarily sells directly to customers through ecommerce and catalogs.

Steve moved to Jackson Hole in 1989 to be a "ski and climbing bum." After working in outdoor retailing for a number of years, he started his first venture, Cloudveil. The company sold outdoor products through wholesale channels to various retailers around the country. The downside to this business model was that the retailers he was selling to were telling the "brand story" to the public, not Steve. After going through several ownership groups, the company headquarters moved out of Jackson Hole.

After a short break, Steve was ready to do it again with a different emphasis and philosophy. He wanted more control over the brand experience, and the only way to do that was to sell directly to customers. His new business model allows him to sell his products to customers all over the world and to tell his brand story the way he wants it told. As a prominent center for outdoor recreation, Jackson Hole is the perfect location for the company. Steve stayed with outdoor apparel after leaving Cloudveil because it's what he knows best. Not only does he have tremendous knowledge of the outdoor apparel industry, but all his team members are also active users of the products. This is another major source of industry knowledge for the company. Steve explains:

> *I think it matters that everyone who works in our company is still an active skier, or a climber, or a kayaker, or a mountain biker, or a trail runner. I think there is an authenticity that comes from using the stuff and getting out there on a very regular basis, and that can't be said of all companies. . . . We get to actively test the products that we are making every day. I can run out from our office and do a tram lap for lunch and check out the fit and function of a*

new jacket that we're trying. . . . The culmination of that leads to better products.

In addition to team members who regularly use the products, Steve has organized a group of Stio Ambassadors. These are athletes, artists, writers, moms, and dads who make the outdoors "an integral part of their lives." They share the company's values, test products, provide feedback, and promote the brand and lifestyle. With Steve's background in outdoor apparel, the vast experience of his team members, and regular input from his Ambassadors, the company has access to ample knowledge about the industry, which leads to better products and a strong competitive advantage.

Mary DeLima also knew a tremendous amount about her industry before starting her business. She has been around horses her whole life. Early on, she decided she wanted to work in the equestrian industry. "It's always been a passion of mine," she says, "something that has always been in my heart." She got a degree from Meredith Manor International Equestrian Centre in West Virginia and has trained with some of the top riders in the field. After 25 years of working at various equestrian centers, she decided she wanted to build her own business. She launched her new venture, DeLima Stables, on her farm in Harrodsburg, Kentucky, in 2004. Mary started small and grew organically, constantly drawing on her experience in the field:

I was actually very blessed and fortunate. I put the word out that I needed some good lesson horses. People called me and said, 'I've got an old horse my kids and grandkids have outgrown and it knows its job. Do you want it?' I said, 'Yes,' and within a couple of weeks I had three lesson horses that I could teach on.

As Mary was teaching lessons, people started bringing horses to her to train, which was a big part of her background. When word got out that she was especially good with young horses, her business really started to grow. Within two years she went from two stalls to 14 and her business was profitable. Today, DeLima Stables is a full-service equestrian center that offers horseback riding lessons to people of all ages, clinics, camps, shows, training, and boarding of horses. Mary holds an awards banquet each year to celebrate the hard work and dedication of her students. Her 25 years of experience in the field have helped her build a very successful business doing what she loves.

Knowledge of Related Industry

Sam Spayd, from Florence, Oregon, doesn't just have a cool name—he owns the coolest airplane I have ever seen, an open cockpit Stearman World War II biplane. The plane was built in January 1944 and was used to train pilots during the war. You can see its blue body, bright yellow double wings, and red-and-white-striped tail from miles away. When you fly with Sam, you wear a leather helmet and goggles, just like the Red Baron. Sam started his sightseeing company, Aero Legends, after flying for United Airlines for 25 years. Early in his career, he flew full time for the Air Force and then in the reserves for a total of 30 years. He flew hundreds of missions, including flights to Korea and Vietnam. One of his more memorable trips was a flight to Korea after the North Koreans captured the USS *Pueblo*. Sam was told he had to get a plane full of supplies over there immediately because the North Koreans might be invading the south. When he got to the airbase, his C-124 was filled with toilet paper for the troops. Sam chuckles as he tells the story.

Sam was diagnosed with stage-four lymphoma in 2001. He beat the disease and got approval from the FAA to fly again. He flew a Boeing 777 for United Airlines until he retired in 2003. Of his bout with cancer, Sam says:

> *The experience of going to the edge of the cliff, looking over, and deciding it wasn't my time to jump off changed the way I live my life. Every day I am around, I do what I want to do. I have joy and pleasure in my life because I do what I choose.*

Sam started Aero Legends after he retired to continue doing what he loves and to share the experience of flying with others. During his tours you see spectacular sights along the Oregon coast, including sea lion caves and the Heceta Head Lighthouse, the most photographed lighthouse in Oregon. Sam has taken this trip more than 300 times. In addition to his Stearman biplane, Sam owns a 1965 Cessna he calls "Buffy." "The reason I have her," he says, "is to get my fix of flying." Here is how Sam summarizes the life he has created for himself:

> *It is great to get up and slip the surly bonds and go flying, either in my Cessna or my Stearman. Every time I do it I get a thrill because I see something I didn't see last time. People go up with me a little apprehensive, and then come back with a huge grin on their face. They are really excited they got to do it because it is such a beautiful part of the country. As long as I am capable, it is what I plan on doing with my life.*

Allen Lim is another successful entrepreneur who is building a remarkable company around his background. While working as a sports scientist and coach for professional cycling teams (Garmin, RadioShack, TIAA-CREF), he spent a lot of time trying to keep his riders from "moaning about their upset bellies." With a Ph.D. in integrative physiology, he knew that prepackaged sports bars and drinks were full of artificial ingredients and high levels of sugar, which was a big part of the problem. Allen started making natural foods and drinks from scratch to keep his riders from getting sick and sustain them through grueling events like the Tour de France, the Tour of Italy, and the Tour of California.

Allen eventually created nutrition and hydration mixes that his athletes loved. They contained more electrolytes, less sugar, and no artificial sweeteners or colors. Each flavor contained real fruit rather than artificial flavorings. "Instead of making an 'orange' drink, I made a drink with real oranges," he explains. The problem was the athletes weren't supposed to use these drinks because they were under contract to use their sponsors' products. But Allen's mixes worked so well that they didn't really care. So he started making his "secret mixes" and putting them in plastic baggies. About this time, Allen realized that endurance cyclists were not the only ones who wanted his mixes. Interest in his products was spreading to racecar drivers, rock climbers, concerned parents, Peace Corps workers, and normal active individuals looking for healthy food and drink alternatives. It was time to start a real business around the mixes.

Allen knew he needed help. He enlisted two friends with the right background and experience: Ian MacGregor and Aaron Foster. Ian is a mechanical engineer and a former professional cyclist; he is the CEO of the company. Aaron is the creative guy: He is an actor, comedian, license plate artist (really), and an avid cyclist. He is the factotum for the company. (I didn't know what it meant either, but it's someone who does a lot of diverse things.) Although these three friends were moving into a slightly different industry, their credibility to build this business was off the charts. Skratch Labs now sells hydration drinks, fruit drops, cookie mixes, cookbooks, and lots of merchandise (cycling kits, triathlon kits, water bottles, T-shirts, hoodies, and hats). The company has gone from doing a few hundred dollars a month to hundreds of thousands of dollars a month. Here is how Allen describes the wild ride they are on:

> *We came into this not because we had business degrees or because we were entrepreneurs. We came into this because we wanted to solve problems in endurance sports, and we wanted control over our lives. . . . There is no way we would be doing this if we weren't having a good time. I think everything we have done at Skratch has started out with the line, 'Wouldn't it be funny if . . .' and then we just fill in the blank. If everything starts out with, 'Wouldn't it be funny if . . .' and then you fill in the blank, things work out because you get engaged at a very intrinsic, unconditional level. Money is a means to an end, not the goal in and of itself.*

Knowledge from Personal Experience

Sheila Kemper Dietrich knew absolutely nothing about manufacturing dinnerware. She also knew very little about marketing weight management products. But she had wrestled with her own weight her entire life. She jokes that she was born overweight. For years she felt it was a burden she just had to bear. Then she started reviewing the research and statistics on obesity. As the executive director of the American Heart Association (AHA) in Colorado, health information was readily available to her—and the news was alarming. The AHA suggested that we are killing ourselves with the food we are eating. The Centers for Disease Control and Prevention declared that many parents are going to outlive their children due to obesity. The American Diabetes Association was focusing on weight gain as a trigger to diabetes and various forms of cancer. This information made Sheila mad:

> *I thought, 'This is insane.' I am a mom of three kids. No mom wakes up in the morning and says, 'How am I going to figure out how to kill my kids with food today?' I mean, it's crazy. We have no idea because we live in this land of bounty and plentitude.*

Sheila went to work on a solution. She learned that the standard dinner plate has increased in size by 50 percent over the years. She knew that eating the right foods was important, but she felt that portion control, or "right sizing," was a critical key to weight management. She searched for portion-control dinnerware but couldn't find what she was looking for. So she created her own:

> *I used my own measuring cups and hand drew these templates. Then I went to the local ceramics shop and hand painted my original sets of Livliga. I made four sets so my husband and daughter could try it out [with me]. Everything was right-sized, and you could see the right portions no matter what you were consuming. . . . And it worked! I lost 50 pounds, my husband lost over 35 pounds, and my daughter lost 25. It's because we were right-sizing our food portions.*

After Sheila's test, her husband said, "Honey, I think you really have something here." And Livliga was born. The company manufactures and sells complete sets of attractive dinnerware that are right-sized. Portions for various food items are clearly displayed on the plates, and bowls and cups are sized for appropriate portions. Sheila's personal weight challenge, combined with information she obtained while working at the AHA, led to an effective solution to weight management. She is currently working hard to spread the Livliga message around the country with great success. Her 2015 sales were five and a half times greater than her sales in 2014. She is growing her business by partnering with professionals in the field, selling on affiliate websites, and private-labeling her products.

Nicole DeBoom is the founder of Skirt Sports, a pioneering company in the women's fitness industry. She had no experience with women's athletic apparel before starting her business but was a serious user of the products. Nicole qualified for the Olympic Swimming Trials in 1988 and went on to swim for Yale University. After graduating, she became a professional triathlete for 11 years. One day on a training run, she had the epiphany that led to Skirt Sports:

> *I glanced at my reflection in a store window. I shook my head and thought to myself, 'I look like a boy again, and I am so tired of it. I just want to look like myself when I am out here working out. I don't want to compromise my personality or my femininity to get my training in.' The word 'pretty' stayed in my mind during that run. I just wanted to feel pretty. I ran home and scribbled the word 'pretty' on a piece of paper, along with a whole bunch of other thoughts on revolutionizing the world of women's fitness clothing.*

Nicole decided to focus on a running skirt, because the skirt is a symbol of femininity. She wore the first skirt she designed during the Ironman Wisconsin and won the race. Her new company was off and running. While launching her new product, she and her team attended an expo in Austin, and a woman walked up to their booth to see what they were doing. After a few minutes she said, "Skirts for running, not going to work." Now, having sold more than $10 million worth of running skirts, Nicole knows her intuition was right. It was based on her experiences as a serious customer in the industry. She created a whole new brand and product category because she couldn't find what she wanted in the marketplace. She made up for her lack of experience in the business by using a host of mentors and team members who knew more than she did.

Sheila and Nicole represent about one-third of the successful entrepreneurs I have interviewed over the years. They have no experience in the industry they start their business in, but they have a great deal of personal experience with the products, services, and problems they are addressing. Once they start their businesses, they become very serious students of the industry. They are usually humble and ready to learn at warp speed. They read books, magazines, and newspapers. They create a brain trust of mentors and advisors who know a lot about the industry. They learn all they can about their competition. And they join associations and user groups. Before long, they know a great deal about their industry—as much as if not more than their competitors.

Sara Blakely, founder of Spanx, is a prominent role model who studiously learned an industry she knew very little about. Sara had a problem in her personal life: She didn't like the bulge that pantyhose caused under her skirt. In addition, she didn't like the muffin-top that formed above tight pantyhose that end below the stomach. She just wanted to look better. Knowing little about the shapewear industry, she spent hours in the library and in hosiery shops. She learned all about the products, patents, and manufacturers. She tried the products on, and then designed something she would love to wear—seamless pantyhose with a higher waist. It was a simple solution to a problem she and all her friends were experiencing.

Sara spent $5,000 starting her business. She did all her research and product development while she was still working full time. She made a cold call to Neiman Marcus, which loved her product. She didn't quit her day job until she had nearly $1 million in orders. Today, Spanx offers 200 "problem-solving products for every body type and budget," including hosiery, bras, panties, bodysuits, swimwear, and even slimming undershirts for men. Sara has completely revolutionized the shapewear industry. Her products are sold in 50 countries worldwide. In 2012, Sara was named the first self-made female billionaire by *Forbes* magazine. All this happened because she had a personal problem, learned an industry better than anyone else, and then solved the problem for herself and every other woman on the planet.

Building a business on what you know is a key factor for success. Your knowledge can come from: 1) working in a specific industry, 2) working in a related industry, or 3) personal experiences you have with products, services, or pain points in an industry. The more you know about your marketplace, the greater your probability for success. The less you know, the greater your chance for failure. It just takes too much time, energy, and money to learn everything by trial and error after you launch a business. So think about opportunities you have seen in your jobs, during your career, and in the personal experiences you have had with various products or services. The next critical step is to find a true business opportunity within the various things you know.

So let's get back to the motorhome in Grangeville, Idaho. It took about a week to figure out exactly what was broken and how to get everything fixed. Dale Weeks, from Dale's Rescue Towing, brought a mechanic to the Bear Den RV Resort, and they replaced the drive train. We had the muffler and tailpipe replaced in Missoula, Montana. A different company in Missoula fixed the gas tank and replaced the house batteries. The electrical system was repaired by Mobile RV Tech in Ennis, Montana. Finally, the greywater tank was repaired by Camping World in Denver, Colorado. As we left the shop in Denver, I told the mechanic how excited I was that our RV was finally fixed. He remarked, "RVs are never fixed. They are houses on a chassis. Something is always going wrong. You just need to know how to maintain and fix them." Great! We still had five weeks to get to the Atlantic Ocean.

The biggest challenge of this breakdown, however, was keeping the bike ride alive. We had companies to visit and entrepreneurs to interview. Many of these visits were planned in advance, so we had to stay on our schedule. The only solution was for Mary and me to go out solo for the rest of the week while Shawn and Jay managed all the repairs. The challenge was that we were in the mountains of Idaho and Montana, where the weather is unpredictable. We would be exposed to the elements, without the ability to jump in the motorhome for shelter, food, or lodging. Oh well, it had to be done. Our plan was to take off from Grangeville and meet them somewhere in Montana later in the week.

Mary and I put our toothbrushes, a change of clothes, and our rain jackets in small backpacks. We rode from Grangeville to Lowell to Lolo to Sula to Dillon on our own. We rode along the beautiful Clearwater River, climbed Lolo Pass with a stuntman from California who played

Bigfoot in *Harry and the Hendersons*, soaked our tired muscles in Lolo Hot Springs, crossed the Continental Divide, and climbed Lost Trail Pass, Chief Joseph Pass, and Big Hole Pass, all above 7,000 feet elevation.

One night it was getting dark and we had nowhere to stay. We were in an open "no man's land" with few options for food and lodging. I called the Sula Country Store and they had some cabins out back. While most of them were "dry" without running water, number 6 was available, which had a bathroom and kitchen. We were still 18 miles away and it was late, so the woman said she would leave the light on, the door open, and the key on the kitchen table. That night we had a glorious hot shower and fell asleep to the sound of animals and the running river. In the morning we had breakfast at the store with three mountain men in their late 80s and 90s. They had all served in the Pacific Theater during World War II. They told us not to worry about a thing because "Obama is going to put a chicken in every pot." Then they laughed heartily.

So our time in the wilderness ended up being an awesome experience. We were handed a lemon, and we made lemonade. This turned out to be a recurring theme on our bike ride across America, not unlike what you face while building a business. You just have to think positively, improvise when needed, keep moving forward, and make things happen.

As we learned later, we could have avoided the disaster on White Bird Hill altogether if we had known more about RV maintenance. Even though the tires had plenty of tread left, they were old. While the motorhome only had 22,000 miles on it, it had been sitting unused for long periods of time. The old tires just couldn't bear the weight of the motorhome *plus* all the extra heavy gear we were carrying. If we had changed them prior to our trip, rather than after the blowout, we would not have been derailed for a week. We just didn't know. Next time we will drive a much lighter van, pull a trailer, and do credit card camping. We know a lot about vans, we know a lot about credit cards, we know a lot about hotels, we know a lot about breakfast buffets, and we know a lot about pulling a trailer, being former boat owners. Next time we will stick with what we know.

REFLECTION

Exploring Your Options

In summary, a strong and motivating purpose is critical to long-term business success, but a variety of opportunities can help you fulfill that purpose. The important thing is to do something you already know a lot about that is consistent with your "Why." The questions below will help you explore experiences and opportunities in your given industry, related industries, and industries you understand as a customer from frequent exposure to the products, services, and pain points. Building on what you know will be critical to your success.

1. What specific industries have you worked in during your career?
2. What problems, pain points, or opportunities have you seen in these industries that could be addressed in a new business?
3. What industries are you most familiar with that are related to the industries you have worked in?
4. What problems, pain points, or opportunities have you seen in these industries that could be addressed in a new business?
5. What specific products, services, or problems are you most familiar with due to frequent use and interaction in these marketplaces?
6. Which of the products, services, or problems you listed in the question above could best be addressed in a new business?
7. Of the business opportunities you listed in questions 2, 4, and 6, which ones are you most qualified to address, based on your experience and skill set?
8. Of the business opportunities you listed in question 7, which ones are most consistent with a strong purpose you would like to achieve?

CHAPTER

4

Launch Opportunities, Not Ideas

"I would see people in the supermarket, I would see them in the hardware store, and they would say, 'You need to start a garbage company. You need to start a garbage company.' After you hear that about a hundred times, the light finally gets full. . . . [So] the opportunity was presented to me, and people believed in me, and I went from there."

—Dave Twombly, founder of Central Coast Disposal

The food company I started developed a full line of frozen dessert products with no fat and reduced calories. We sold these products in retail stores around the western United States. Every month I got phone calls from people who wanted to sell our products in their businesses, restaurants, convenience stores, hotels, delis, casinos, etc. I always told them no. Our proprietary products were the heart of our retail business. We didn't want to dilute our brand or our sales. Then one week I got calls from two major players who wanted to sell our products: Hardee's and Maverik Country Stores. With multiple locations around the west, these two accounts would be worth half a million dollars a year with an attractive profit margin. I said no anyway.

But I couldn't get these two companies off my mind. Then the lights came on. I would create a new brand, enter the wholesale market, and sell to these two accounts and every other business that wanted our product line. I already had a super team, corporate offices, a production facility, existing distribution, and strong financial resources. It was a no-brainer, so that's exactly what we did. I called Hardee's and Maverik back and sold them on the concept. They loved the idea. Within a few weeks we had a new brand and were in production. The earnings from these initial accounts allowed us to bring in a sales executive and continue building our new brand. This venture quickly became a multimillion-dollar company.

A True Business Opportunity

Our new wholesale company was what I call a "true business opportunity." It contained five critical components required for any successful venture. First, the need for the product was clearly there, from all the calls I was getting (NEED). Second, we obviously had the expertise and credibility to launch this venture (EXPERIENCE). Third, we had all the resources we would need to get started—people, production, distribution, and funds (RESOURCES). Fourth, we had customers who were committed to buying our product (CUSTOMERS). And fifth, we knew the business model was sound from being in the industry—pricing, cost of goods, gross margin, and profit margin (MODEL). It was a perfect opportunity, not an anemic idea or pipe dream.

Over the years, I have seen a lot of entrepreneurs succeed and a lot of them fail. The ones who succeed generally have these five components in place before launching their venture. While the five factors may not be as strong as they were with our new wholesale food business, the stronger they are, the greater your chances for success. The less these factors exist, the higher your probability for failure. Let's discuss these five components of a true opportunity in more detail.

Genuine Need

True business opportunities meet needs or solve pain points people have in their lives. The best way to discover these needs and pain points is by being intimately involved in a particular field or industry. As we discussed in Chapter 3, most successful entrepreneurs have worked in the industry they start their business in, in a related industry, or are very familiar with the products, services, and problems through personal experience. They discover a need and verify it through firsthand observation. You generally don't discover pressing needs by joining a think tank, learning how to brainstorm, or sitting in a university class.

I can't tell you how many aspiring entrepreneurs I have met who have fallen in love with an idea; it's clever, cute, and even fun. The only problem is that no one needs it, wants it, or is willing to pay for it. I tell them, "You have a great solution—now you need to find a problem it solves." It is far easier to do it the other way around: Find the problem first, and then create the solution. If you need the product personally, that's great. If all your friends, family members, colleagues, and work associates need it, that's even better. You will see how the role models that follow discovered the need they are addressing from being involved in the marketplace and had ample evidence that people wanted their product.

Credible Experience

We have already discussed the importance of building on what you know. Knowing the products, services, and problems in an industry not only helps you avoid the pitfalls of trial-and-error learning, but it also gives interested parties the confidence that you are the right person to build this business. Your experience and credibility are very important to potential team members, investors, customers, suppliers, and strategic partners. If you don't have the skills and experience to build your business, you will be fighting an uphill battle. When this is the case, it's best to find advisors, partners, and team members who can fill in the gaps in your skill set. In the end, you and your team will need to have the experience and credibility necessary to build your business.

Adequate Resources

Many would-be entrepreneurs think they need money to start their new venture—no money, no business. Actually, successful entrepreneurs use a host of other resources to get started; they work from home, find mentors and advisors, use free software, acquire used equipment, barter and trade, partner with their first customers, obtain credit from suppliers, and borrow before they rent or buy. The important thing is to determine what your new venture requires, and then go out and find the resources you need to get started. You don't necessarily need funding, but you do need resources.

Buying Customers

You will see that the role models who follow had customers committed to buying their products or services as soon as they launched their ventures. Dave Twombly had customers waiting for him to launch his garbage company. Patrick Hayden already had customers buying his firearms and accessories. And Joanne McCall sold her first contract to her employer prior to launching her agency. When you have specific customers who are willing to buy your product as soon as you launch your venture, you have the ultimate validation of your solution, immediate sales, and early cash flow from which to grow. Selling your products or services prior to your launch is always a great strategy. If you can't do it, you may not be ready to go.

Sound Business Model

Your business model is the way you will make money in your venture. It includes your sources of revenue, pricing, costs of goods sold, gross margin, operating costs, and profit margin—essentially the elements of an income statement. It answers the following questions:

1. Who are my various customer groups? (revenue sources)
2. How much will they pay for my products? (revenue)
3. What will it cost me to make these products? (cost of goods)
4. How much money do I make from each sale? (gross margin)
5. What are my expenses for running this business? (operating costs)
6. After all costs, how much does the business make? (profit margin)

The best businesses have multiple sources of revenue, competitive pricing, a 50 percent or better gross margin, and a 10 to 20 percent profit margin. If your numbers aren't this attractive, it will be difficult to survive. So make sure all the numbers work before launching your venture.

I call these five components for identifying true business opportunities the NERCM model (pronounced *ner-come*):

N = Need
E = Experience
R = Resources
C = Customers
M = Model

When people come to me with business ideas and ask what to do next, I tell them to "NERCM." In other words: 1) gather tangible evidence that people really need your product, 2) evaluate your experience and credibility, and fill in the missing pieces, 3) cobble together the resources you will need to get started, 4) find customers who are willing to buy your product as soon as you launch, and 5) make sure all the numbers in your business model work. When these factors fall into place, it is time to go. If these factors are not in place, starting your business would be premature.

The failure rate for new businesses is very high: 50 percent fail within five years and 70 percent fail within ten years. I strongly believe this is because people launch ideas, not opportunities. When you launch an idea, you burn through all of your resources before you can figure things out, gain traction, and produce profit.

Our Opportunistic Entrepreneurs

Let's now turn to some of the role models we discovered across America. Notice the degree to which the five components of true business opportunities—NERCM—were present in their new ventures.

Dave and Lynne Twombly

Florence, Oregon, had always had two garbage companies. "The city wanted it that way," Dave explains. "They believed in the American

Dream; they believed in competition." But then a large corporation came to town and bought both of them. Dave had worked for one of these businesses for nine years. He and Lynne moved to Florence to live on his family's 20-acre farm when Lynne was pregnant with their third child. Dave was offered the job with the garbage company a few days after they arrived. After nine years, he took a job as a foreman at a construction company because he needed to make more money to fund his children's education and his own retirement.

After the big corporation moved in, people were constantly telling Dave that the town needed another garbage company. They didn't like having one business dominate the market, and they didn't like the service they were receiving from the corporate giant. Dave heard this again and again, everywhere he went. After dozens of people told him they would support his new business, he knew he had a true opportunity.

The first thing Dave and Lynne had to do was secure the resources required to start their company—they needed $360,000 for the equipment. They were able to borrow some of the money from family members and the rest through leases with liens against the equipment. Several people in town provided these leases at good rates because they thought it was a good investment. Dave's background wasn't just important in securing the funding—it was critical to his overall success:

> *I came up against things that were a surprise to me, and I was in an industry I knew. If I hadn't had information to appease the city, the Department of Environmental Quality, and the Department of Transportation, I wouldn't have made it. So whenever anyone tells me, 'I want to start a business,' the first thing out of my mouth is, 'Make sure you do something that you know.' . . . So when you go into business, you need to have as much information as possible so you don't have to learn things later.*

Dave and Lynne have now owned Central Coast Disposal for more than 15 years. Dave runs the operation, and Lynne manages the office. They have added services, purchased land, and built a 9,600-square-foot facility. Their business has succeeded because the need clearly existed, Dave had experience in the field, they had the resources they required, customers were anxious to buy from them, and the business model was sound as a result of Dave's previous experience. It was a true business opportunity.

Gary Delp

Gary Delp loves his work. "I can't think of any other form of employment that would give me greater satisfaction," he says. His company, Heritage Timber, dismantles old buildings, such as sawmills, barns, cabins, houses, and businesses, and then sells the reclaimed wood. His customers build homes, lodges, bridges, breweries, and other types of rustic businesses.

Gary is from New York. He moved to Missoula, Montana, to attend the University of Montana, but he quickly realized that school was not his thing and spent the next year hitchhiking around the country. He had fallen in love with Montana, so he went back to Missoula looking for work. He called a temporary employment agency, and they found him a job with two guys who were tearing down an old sawmill. It was a large, timber-frame building—nearly 40,000 square feet—so it took a while to complete the project. It was on this job that Gary learned the business of dismantling old buildings and selling the reclaimed materials.

Gary saw a great opportunity in this field. He knew there were lots of old mills, cabins, homes, barns, bridges, and businesses in Montana. He felt there was enough work to sustain him long term. So he gave one of the partners on the job $5,000 for his share of the business. After a while, the other partner moved on, and Gary began growing the company, Heritage Timber. Here is how the business works: Gary finds a structure that needs to come down; sometimes he gets the materials for free, and other times he pays for the building. In the early days, he would find a buyer for the materials before committing to the project. It was a perfect opportunity! When he had a paying customer, he only risked his time. Most of these buyers were wholesale customers who were using the wood on projects with *their* customers. Since the buildings Gary was dismantling were very large, he was sending semi loads of wood to these jobs. As the business matured, Gary began accepting projects without committed buyers and storing the wood for future sales.

In 2008, Gary married his girlfriend, Becky, and she started working in the business. Her background was in marketing, so she built an attractive website and started promoting the products more aggressively to retail customers, which yielded a higher price than selling the wood wholesale. Demand from retail buyers has grown significantly in recent years. Gary now has three young children and hopes to involve them in the business as they grow older. Here is how he summarizes the opportunity he has developed for himself and his family:

> *I love the idea of a family business, so I'd like to work with my kids if it's something they are interested in. But I really love the work on a day-to-day basis. I mean, we keep thousands of tons of material out of the landfill. We give great green alternatives for people building homes and businesses. If we just continue that for the next however many years, I'd be quite happy.*

Don and Bonnie Moran

Don had a serious problem: He was basically unemployable. At least that was what Bonnie told him when they were in high school. She made sure he graduated, but she told him he would have to start his own business someday in order to survive. All Don wanted to do was become a mechanic, so he took a job working for TWA. Of this experience, he says:

> *There were five strikes while I was there. The union hated the company, and the company hated the union. If you screwed up an airplane for the night, you were a hero. That wasn't where I wanted to spend my life; there was zero pride in the work.*

Later in life, Don and Bonnie sold their home and shop and bought a Country Coach Motorhome. They were living in an RV community in Yuma, Arizona. People kept telling Don he should start an RV repair company: he owned an RV, lived in a community of RV owners, and was an excellent mechanic when anyone needed repairs. He decided it was a good idea. Twenty years earlier, he had built a mobile repair truck that his son was now using. He called his son and told him he needed his truck back, and started his RV repair business. Since Yuma is stiflingly hot during the summer, Don spent those months going away to every school he could find to become a factory technician for a variety of motorhomes, parts, and systems. As soon as he was certified, the factories would send him work from people who had problems in his area.

One summer Don and Bonnie stopped at an RV park in Ennis, Montana, on their way home from Yellowknife, Canada. They fell in love with the area, the city, and the people. Unfortunately, Don became very sick while they were in Ennis:

> *I ended up in the hospital; my potassium was zero, which is a heart attack. No waiting room, no paperwork, no nothing. They took me in and started working on me. It was a brand-new hospital, and I told Bonnie, 'This is where I want to die.'*

Don and Bonnie now have their mobile repair business, Mobile RV Tech, in Ennis. They bought some land, built a shop, and park their Country Coach Motorhome beside it. Don has all the work he can handle. The day we met him he had three appointments, but he was willing to squeeze us in to repair our electrical system, a casualty from the incident on White Bird Hill. While any mechanic can work on motorhomes, Don specializes in the big expensive buses, so he brings a lot of money to town. These visitors shop in the stores, eat in the restaurants, and occasionally buy property. The people in Ennis are very happy to have Don and Bonnie in town. When business slows down in the winter, Don makes decorative art out of horseshoes. He can also work on snowmobiles and anything else with an engine. The true business opportunity he launched—with a genuine need, experience, resources, customers, and a sound business model—has provided a very attractive lifestyle.

Melanie Marlow and Mike Domeyer

Melanie worked on a cow ranch for 20 years. The population of the town was 32. The closest grocery store was an hour and a half away.

One year Melanie was injured and could no longer do ranching. She had been sewing for years and saw a new opportunity:

> *I started sewing when I was nine years old. I was given a sewing machine for my birthday. My father makes handmade boots, so I have been around leather and cloth and sewing for most of my life. I am very comfortable with it. It just feels right.*

Melanie started sewing for her family, friends, neighbors, and "everyone." Because she was so far away from civilization, she had to take her products where the people were, which meant vending on the road. She went to major shows like Cheyenne Frontier Days and the National Rodeo Finals in Las Vegas. That's how she met Mike.

Mike also grew up on ranches. When he was nine years old he helped his uncle haul hay. One day he was driving a wagon full of hay, caught the wheel on a fence post, and did some serious damage. His uncle thought he needed to learn another skill, and said, "Well, it's time you learn to sew." So Mike learned to sew, but he continued with ranching and ended up managing a guest ranch in California. He also got a pilot's license, an instructor rating, and continued to work with leather. Like Melanie, he eventually took his products on the road and got heavily involved with the Single Action Shooting Society (SASS). He made high-quality leather holsters for many of the competitors.

Melanie and Mike met at a "state shoot" in Idaho, where their spaces were right next to each other. They started talking and decided to pool their inventory for their next show in Las Vegas. That was the beginning of their partnership. As they worked together for the next few years, the costs of vending on the road—gas, lodging, booth fees—went up significantly, and they decided it made more sense to start a new business in a retail location. The rent for a retail storefront was far less than their vending costs, and they already had the tools, equipment, supplies, experience, and credibility. Most important, they had lots of buying customers. People they met on the road were constantly contacting them for custom-made products, and each satisfied customer told two or three more people about them. They had all the components of a true business opportunity—NERCM.

Shasta Leatherworks is located in Prineville, Oregon. Their first space was above a clothing store, and the rent was free! This got them off to a good start. They later moved to a very attractive location right on Main Street. Today, they make a wide variety of stunning custom leather goods, such as clothes, holsters, chaps, vests, belts, purses, wallets, and briefcases. People see their products online and then have a detailed conversation with Mike or Melanie about dimensions, functions, and colors. Many of their customers are on the East Coast, particularly in Florida. They have sent products as far away as North Pole, Alaska and Athens, Greece. Here is how Melanie describes their life in Prineville:

> *I absolutely love it here: the climate, the things to do, the recreation, and the people are fabulous! There are no strangers here. You walk into any store and they are happy you are there. It's just a really nice place.*

Patrick Hayden

After graduating from college, Patrick and his father bought an old general store in Bardstown, Kentucky. It was run down and doing badly; they bought it primarily for the real estate. The store was an old-fashioned general mercantile that carried a wide variety of products. It was run so poorly that some of the food on the shelves was two years out of date. The store once had an ATF license to sell firearms, but it had been revoked due to poor record keeping.

Patrick ran the store for a few years and built it back up. But he realized that small-town general stores were dying as Walmart and other big boxes were moving into rural areas. During this time, Patrick renewed the store's ATF license and sold 300 guns the first year. There was clearly a need for a high-quality firearms and hunting store in the area. As firearm sales continued to grow, and people began coming from farther and farther away, Patrick knew it was time to launch his new venture, the Kentucky Gun Co. He had strong evidence the need existed, experience and credibility, the required resources, buying customers, and a proven business model—NERCM.

For the next seven or eight years, Patrick only sold products out of his retail location in Bardstown, but he developed a customer base across the country. He knew it was time to start selling online. Kentucky Gun Co. now sells 30,000 guns a year along with optics, ammunition, holsters, belts, and all accessories. The growth of this true business opportunity has been remarkable. Online sales now account for 80 percent of the total business. Here is how Patrick summarizes this wild ride:

> *I don't wake up and think, 'Doggone, I have to go to work.' I actually enjoy going to work. It is not a job, fortunately. It's a passion. It's a hobby. And luckily, it pays the bills at the same time. I work with great people. I live in a great town. . . . I think I am about as close as I can get to the American Dream.*

Joanne McCall

One of the most critical elements of a true business opportunity is customers who are ready to buy your product or service right now. Even if you only have one committed customer, it's a good starting point. That's what Joanne had when she started her public relations and visibility agency, McCall Media Group.

Joanne worked in radio broadcasting for a number of years. She actually got her start in the Junior Achievement Program in high school; she produced a biweekly show for a local radio station and absolutely loved it. She went on to work at a number of radio stations. Her favorite part was interviewing authors, speakers, entrepreneurs, and business owners. When publicists would contact her to schedule these interviews, Joanne would always think, "I can do that." She knew what broadcasters wanted from being in the field and felt she would be a great publicist. She kept that thought in the back of her mind.

After years in broadcasting, Joanne took a job as the PR director at a conference and retreat center. Six months into the job, her executive director got a major book contract with Bantam Doubleday Dell. The publisher wanted her executive director to go on a 25-city tour to promote the book, and Joanne was asked to plan and organize the tour.

She quickly realized that it would be very difficult to do her current job and successfully manage her boss's book tour. She didn't feel she could do both jobs justice. Here is what she did:

> *I set up a meeting with the executive director. I went in and handed her my resignation, then handed her a proposal. I said, 'I'm going out on my own. I want you to be my first client.' She blinked about three times and knew there was no one at that point who could step in and take off with this. So she said, 'OK,' and that's what launched me.*

Joanne teaches us a valuable lesson about turning your employer into your first client. As more and more organizations start outsourcing services to reduce costs, this is a great way to start your own business. Many of the entrepreneurs I have interviewed over the years found their first customer this way. Joanne went on to manage the 25-city tour and promote the book. Within a few months she had other clients as well. She has now been promoting authors, artists, musicians, and celebrities for nearly 20 years. In addition, she helps businesses gain greater visibility through a variety of media strategies. She has a full stable of strategic partners—editors, ghostwriters, publicists, graphic designers, and web developers whom she uses for various projects. Here is what motivates her to do all she can to help people promote their projects and businesses:

> *My sister passed away from a very rare form of cancer. Two days before she passed, she said to me, 'I can't believe I didn't go after my dreams,' because she was a great artist. She said, 'I always had an excuse. I didn't have the money. I didn't have the time. I'd wait until this happened.' Then she was out of tomorrows. I can't tell you how that broke my heart. I reflected on that a lot and made a decision that if anybody wanted to get their message out there about their business, I would help them do that.*

Applying the NERCM Model

Most of the successful entrepreneurs I have interviewed over the years tell a similar story. First they discover a need that is not being addressed in the marketplace or a better way to meet a need that is being addressed (better quality, better price, better service, etc.). While contemplating their discovery, they realize they are uniquely positioned to meet this need. They have the skills, experience, contacts, training, and credibility. Next, they assemble the resources they need to start the venture: a prototype, advisors, equipment, supplies, funds, etc. Then they find customers who are willing to buy their product as soon as their company launches. Finally, they confirm that their business model works—NERCM.

Compare this scenario to the aspiring entrepreneur who decides to start a business, quits his job, conjures up an idea while sitting on the couch, and tries to push his way into an unfamiliar industry. I'm sure you get the point: The first example is a true business opportunity and the second is a pipe dream. So make sure you have a true opportunity before you launch your venture. The worst thing you can do is launch prematurely and become a failure statistic. It may not be that your concept wasn't sound, but that you jumped the gun before you were ready.

Finally, the NERCM model is also relevant when you launch a new product or service in an existing company. For example, our bike ride across America was not just a wild and crazy adventure; it was also an opportunity to develop our own business. It allowed us to obtain remarkable information on entrepreneurship, develop new training programs for our customers, gain excellent publicity for our company, and create new films and a book to sell in our market. We had ample evidence that this was a great business opportunity. We get calls from aspiring entrepreneurs nearly every day. We have the experience and credibility to teach entrepreneurship. We have all the resources we need to create new products and services. We have customers who agreed to buy our products on Kickstarter before we started our tour. We know our business model works from previous experience. All the components of the NERCM model were present—it was a true opportunity. It was also one of the most thrilling things we have ever done. So the NERCM model can also help you assess new opportunities within an existing business.

REFLECTION

Assessing the Five Factors

In sum, you now have a strong purpose for your business. You have knowledge and experience with certain industries, products, and services. You may even have several business concepts you are contemplating. Now you need to make sure you launch a true business opportunity, not just an idea. The questions below will help you determine if the five components of the NERCM model are working in your favor. The more these factors are present in your new venture, the greater your probability for success.

1. What specific need or "pain point" does your product or service meet that is not being adequately addressed? (NEED)
2. What tangible evidence do you have that people will actually buy your product or service? (NEED)
3. What experiences have you had with the products or services in this industry? (EXPERIENCE)
4. What makes you uniquely qualified to launch this business? (EXPERIENCE)
5. What specific resources will you need to launch your new company? (RESOURCES)
6. How will you acquire the resources you need to launch this business? (RESOURCES)
7. What customer groups are most likely to buy your product or service after you launch your venture? (CUSTOMERS)
8. What specific individuals or companies are committed to buy your product or service right when you launch? (CUSTOMERS)
9. What are the key components of your business model: pricing, cost of goods, gross margin, operating costs, and profit margin? (MODEL)
10. What evidence do you have that these numbers will actually hold in the real world? (MODEL)

CHAPTER

5

Develop Your Supporting Cast

"I think it is huge having a supportive cast. . . . People want to help people, right? That's just our nature. I think the more you ask for help, the more help you are going to get. . . . I was really lucky to find a lot of people, and they have stuck around."

—Amy Gardner, founder of Scarpa

Most of my friends who start cycling tell me they don't want to draft behind anyone—they are afraid they will crash. I always smile and say, "No problem, you don't have to if you don't want to." Next we go on a few long rides and our new non-drafting friend struggles to keep up. Finally, he or she says, "Sorry, I'm just not as fast as you guys." I reply, "I know you don't want to draft behind us, but why not try it just once and see what happens?" I then explain the concept of drafting—stay about a foot behind the rider in front of you, keep your eyes on his tire, don't slow down or stop unexpectedly—and we give it a try. Surprise! Our new rider stays with the group and is hooked. That's all it takes.

Drafting is critical in long-distance cycling. You form a pace line and stay close to each other. The person in front holds a steady pace and breaks the wind for the other riders in the line. The riders in back use 20 to 30 percent less energy and get a nice rest. After a couple of minutes, the lead rider pulls to the side, drifts to the back of group, and the next person in line takes the lead. If you switch leaders every five minutes and have six riders in your group, you only take two five-minute shifts out front every hour. The rest of the time you conserve energy. This allows your team to ride farther, faster, and more efficiently. A single rider fighting the wind alone can never go as far or as fast as a well-calibrated team working together.

This same phenomenon works in nature. Geese instinctively fly in a "V" formation to conserve energy. It is estimated that the geese in the back of the "V" can reduce their wind resistance by up to 65 percent and increase their range by 70 percent. Supposedly, the geese honk during their journey to encourage their leader up front: *Way to go, George! You are doing a great job! Keep up the hard work!* At regular intervals they change positions so every goose takes a turn out front. They can go a lot farther and faster when they work together.

Teamwork was critical on our 4,000-mile bike ride across America. Since I was riding the full distance and the others were rotating in, we had three squads: the mountain squad, the all-terrain squad, and the flat and downhill squad. I weigh 145 pounds, so I am a pretty good climber, and Mary is a mountain goat at 105 pounds. She and I generally rode together on the steepest hills. Jay is an excellent all-terrain rider at 175 pounds. He is very strong on long distances over hills, flat land, and downhill. Jay pulled me along during much of the trip. He was not only our workhorse with video production, but also on our rides. Shawn is 6'2" and weighs 215 pounds. He rides downhill like a mortar launched from a cannon. He was our flat land and downhill specialist. Riding behind him was like following a big blocker on a football team.

Initially, Shawn and I had the most difficulty working together. With a 70-pound weight difference, we were not very compatible on the hills. He would crank the pedals like a maniac at the start of each downhill, and the gap between us would grow significantly. When the uphill started, I would easily pass him and have to wait for him at the top. I was using too much energy trying to catch him on the downhill, and he was using too much energy trying to stay with me on the uphill. We were getting very little advantage from riding together, so we had a friendly conversation about our dilemma. After that, he slowed down on the downhill and made sure I was right on his back tire. I slowed down on the uphill and pulled him to the top. We finally stayed together all day long on a 101-mile ride, and we both felt great! So it took a while to hone our team skills, but by the time we got to Kansas we were humming like a fine-tuned machine. We enjoyed the constant rolling hills, the beautiful farms, the Barbed Wire Capital of the World (La Crosse), and the Prairie Chicken Capital of the World (Cassoday)—all while cruising along at maximum efficiency. When we worked together, the long days were not that difficult.

Just as in long-distance cycling, teamwork is critical to building a successful business. As we have discussed in previous chapters, you now have an engaging purpose for starting your new venture. You have explored all the experiences you have had with jobs, products, and services. You have selected a true business opportunity rather than an idea. Now it's time to build your cast of supporting characters. The successful entrepreneurs we met across America build three types of teams: 1) they engage a "brain trust" of mentors and advisors who coach them for free, 2) they build a team of partners who join them in the venture, and 3) they develop strategic partnerships with individuals and businesses that play critical roles for the company. Nearly all of our entrepreneurs built a brain trust and strategic partnerships, even if they were operating a solo company. If they were growing a larger business, they also built a team of full-time partners. Let's discuss these three types of teams in more detail.

Building Your Brain Trust

Thriving entrepreneurs turn to a brain trust of mentors to help them build their business. These mentors might be friends, family members, neighbors, teachers, entrepreneurs, former colleagues, and business owners. Savvy advisors can help you with every phase of business development. They can offer expertise, provide resources, eliminate road blocks, introduce important contacts, and help you avoid serious mistakes during your journey. Nearly all the entrepreneurs we met across America have developed a brain trust of mentors who assist them with a wide variety of issues. The following are some examples.

Omer Orian

Omer loves people, food, and the restaurant business. Most of all, he loves liege waffles, waffles made with chunks of pearl sugar that according to him create a heavenly texture and flavor that is to die for. Omer spent four years in Belgium with his family when he was a child, and one of his first memories is of a liege waffle. His kindergarten teacher gave him one for not "causing a ruckus" that day. From that time on, he knew he wanted to make liege waffles for people in his own restaurant someday.

As Omer got older, he spent a lot of time traveling around Latin America with his brother Dave. They would work in restaurants in Northern California's Bay Area to earn money and then visit countries like Peru, Guatemala, Honduras, Chile, and Brazil. When they ran out of money, they would go back to the Bay Area for more work. On one trip back home, they bought a Honda Prelude for $1,000 and started driving north. When they got to Eugene, Oregon, they "couch surfed" for a month and fell in love with the people, city, and relaxed environment. It was the perfect place to open their first waffle eatery, Off the Waffle.

Omer and Dave lived in a house that was zoned for commercial use. Since they had no money to rent a restaurant space, they opened their shop in their living room. They quickly built a huge following of raving fans. After eight months, the city informed them their house was not up to code for a restaurant. They would have to remodel, close down, or move to a new location. Since they now had cash flow and a large customer base, they decided to open their first real brick-and-mortar restaurant in south Eugene. This was in 2009, and the restaurant was a huge success:

> *The minute we opened up, the lines were out the door. It was apparent we would not be able to serve all the people who wanted to eat at our restaurant out of that location.*

In 2012 the brothers opened a second restaurant in downtown Eugene, and two years later they opened a third in Portland. When it was clear the business was going to grow, their father, Shimon, and their sister, Vered, joined their team. Omer believes their success is a result of fresh and organic ingredients, a fun and relaxed atmosphere, excellent customer service, and help from mentors and advisors along the way. Even though the brothers knew a lot about the restaurant business, they relied heavily on other people:

> *We are pretty quick to call friends and family and neighbors and even people we don't know to ask for help. I can call business owners in Eugene, and they will go out of their way to help me. Here is a really good example. My buddy Tim from Vanilla Jill's, the best frozen yogurt I have ever had in my life, is a general contractor by trade. I was doing some projects around my shop and was in way over my head. I called him and said, 'Tim, I need your help.' He was right there and stayed with me that night until four in the morning. We removed an old Baskin-Robbins freezer that was left in the store. It turned out he needed some of the panels for a project he was working on, so that was pretty cool.*

Justin Gold

Justin Gold also used mentors and advisors to launch his wildly successful company, Justin's. Justin is a vegetarian who gets a lot of his protein from nuts. He found out peanut butter is pretty easy to make. "You take peanuts, put them in a food processor, turn it on, and 30 seconds later you have peanut butter," he says. He started adding blueberries, coconut, cinnamon, white chocolate, and other ingredients; putting the mixtures in jars; and storing them in his cupboard. His roommates loved his creations and started calling them "Justin's." This was his first indication that he really had something.

Justin decided to sell his products at the local farmers market in Boulder, Colorado. He made larger batches at a catering company that let him use their kitchen in the evenings and on weekends. His products were such a big hit he decided to approach Whole Foods. He made friends with the buyer and learned how to comply with all the USDA and FDA packing and labeling requirements. When his products were ready, the buyer gave him a chance. He started with one Whole Foods store, then three, and then 30.

During this time, Justin was still working at a backpacking store and doing a lot of mountain biking. One day he was craving a shot of protein instead of a sugary gel, and he had an epiphany. He thought, "How come no one is putting nut butters into squeeze packs?" That was his next big project. Before long he had a strong tandem relationship between his jars of nut butters and his squeeze packs. People could now sample a flavor in a small squeeze pack before buying a whole jar. And, of course, the fitness community loved the squeeze packs.

Today, Justin's products are sold in jars, squeeze packs, and peanut butter cups in stores like HEB, Jewel-Osco, Kroger, Publix, Safeway, Target, Wegmans, and Whole Foods Market. Flavors include almond, hazelnut, maple, honey, vanilla, and chocolate. Justin has been recognized as Entrepreneur of the Year by Ernst & Young, and his company was ranked in the Inc. 5000 Fastest Growing Companies list in 2012 and 2013. In the end, Justin attributes his success to all the mentors who have helped him build his company:

> *As revolutionary as I thought I was, I'm really just selling a product into grocery food stores, and there are a lot of people who have done that before. Lots of these folks, by the time they reach a certain level of success, really want to help. So I was able to find a network of these mentors who gave me a lot of free advice. They were able to help me make the right decisions, avoid some potentially devastating mistakes, and keep me motivated and inspired. These mentors have been such a huge part of my life. I call them for everything.*

Justin has called on more than ten significant mentors while building his business. They have each helped him with specific things: designing his label, formulating his recipes, marketing his products, building his sales team, and forecasting cash flow, to name a few.

Justin has become a master at finding and enlisting mentors in his cause:

> *You pick your heroes and chart a course to get to them. Once you get an introduction, you want to maintain a friendship. . . . I found out that one of my mentors loves to go on morning hikes. So I asked him, 'How about I meet you at the Mount Sanitas Trailhead and we'll go hiking tomorrow at 7:30* A.M.*?' And he's like, 'That's funny, that's where and when I usually go hiking.' I'm like, 'Perfect, I will meet you there!' So I made it really easy for them to meet with me. That friendship can blossom into mentorship and you can ask them to be on your advisory board. . . . Three of my favorite mentors are now on my board, and I have a regular relationship with them. So I really lean on my mentors for a lot.*

Amy Gardner

Amy loves nice shoes. As a student at the University of Virginia, she was surprised there wasn't a high-end women's shoe store in Charlottesville. She and other women with her taste had to go elsewhere to find what they wanted. So after graduating from college, Amy opened Scarpa, a women's shoe and accessory boutique in Charlottesville. Although she knew a lot about elegant shoes, she was not familiar with the shoe industry. Her solution was to find some mentors and advisors who were:

> *I'm fortunate there are a lot of really supportive people in a small town—that's one of the perks of small towns. So I took classes at the community college in accounting and marketing. I engaged the Small Business Development Center, which is a state-funded program. And I used the resources of SCORE—Service Corps of Retired Executives. I met a great mentor there, Joe Geller. His father had a shoe manufacturing company and a store in Boston. Joe had retired from there, and he was amazing. His name opened a lot of doors when I went to New York.*

Amy has successfully operated her retail business for more than 20 years. She also sells her products on the internet. Amy continues to use advisors and mentors when needed. She recently hired a coach to help her with some difficult issues. Here is her advice on how to best use mentors:

> *I think it is huge not to be needy, but to know how to ask for help. You have to be respectful of people's time. You have to know enough not to ask the most basic questions. Research enough so you are not wasting someone's time when you go to them. Do the hard work along the way so they can see what progress you are making. If you are not following through and taking it seriously, then you are wasting their time and they are going to give up.*

So building a brain trust of advisors has been critical for Omer, Justin, and Amy. Omer needed help with construction issues, Justin needed help designing labels and formulating recipes, and Amy needed to make contacts with shoe-industry suppliers in New York. These business builders would not be as successful as they are without their brain trust. The other entrepreneurs we interviewed tell similar stories about the vital role mentors have played in their success. Here are a few brief quotes from people you have already met.

> Nicole DeBoom, founder of Skirt Sports: *I think that learning from other people's mistakes, and most importantly, their successes, is the only way to learn in your business. When I started out I had coffee meetings ten times a week. I was really wired. I just started picking people's brains. So I believe 100 percent in mentors.*

> Steve Sullivan, founder of Stio: *I have a broad set of informal friends and mentors out there, and I think that's one of the most critical things: to try to mine good information from good people. I regularly communicate with a half-dozen people about aspects of our business, whether it's staffing or financials or product or factories. That's one of the advantages I have starting this brand.*

> Allen Lim, founder of Skratch Labs: *I think we have been pretty blessed to have so many amazing advisors. These are people who actually care for us. When your friends, family, and people who have*

known you for a long time step in and tell you something, you better listen. To that end, we have been phenomenally lucky to have great advisors. This list is pretty endless.

The larger your brain trust, the more successful you will be in your business. So how do you find these people? I have put together a simple process from the hundreds of entrepreneurs I have interviewed over the years. Here are the basic steps:

Step 1: Complete a detailed inventory of the critical skills needed in your business. For example, some businesses are very labor intensive, while others are sales intensive; some require manufacturing and quality control, and others require ecommerce, information technology, and social media. What critical skills does your business need? The assessment tool at the end of this chapter will help you complete this step.

Step 2: Conduct an honest evaluation of your own skills relative to the critical skills needed in your business. In other words, what are your strengths and weaknesses relative to your profile of required skills? The assessment tool at the end of this chapter will also help you complete this step. It will reveal the gaps you need to fill with advisors and team members.

Step 3: Select one or two primary mentors who know you well and are willing to help. These are often friends, family members, or colleagues who are willing to take your calls and meet with you regularly. It's best if they understand business, have a large pool of contacts, and are passionate about what you are doing.

Step 4: Meet with your primary mentors and review the list of critical skills needed in your business. Discuss your own strengths and weaknesses relative to this profile. Ask if they know people who have the required skills you lack. See if they will contact these people on your behalf or at least allow you to use their name as a reference.

Step 5: Meet with all the referrals you get and explain what you are doing. See if these people are willing to talk occasionally as questions arise. Be prepared for these meetings, don't waste people's time, and always ask if there is anything you can do for them in return. Your goal is to build mutually beneficial relationships. In addition, when needs arise ask these advisors if they know others who may be willing to help with specific issues. Figure 5–1 shows how one primary mentor can lead to six potential advisors for your company.

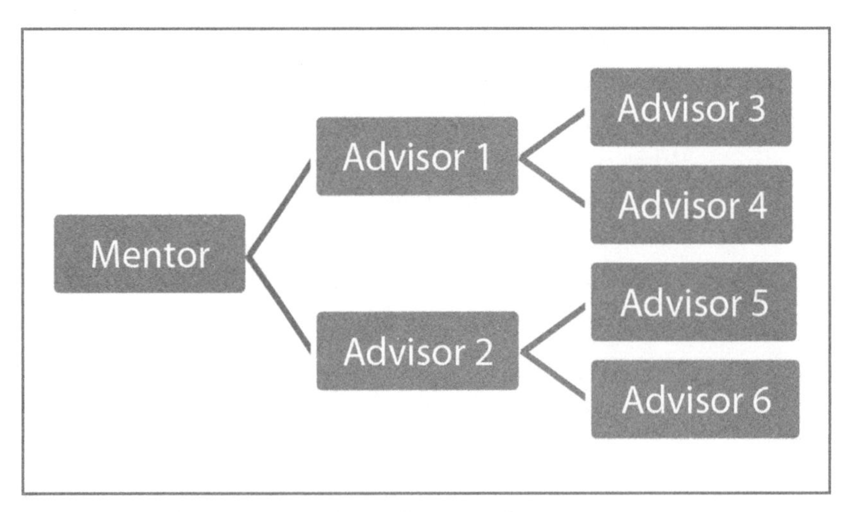

Figure 5–1: **Finding Advisors Through Networking**

Building Your Core Team

Mary and I ran our frozen dessert business by ourselves until we had three stores and 30 employees. Although we had three great store managers, it was clear we would eventually need more coverage in the field than we could provide. So we sat down and discussed the characteristics of a great general manager. This person had to "get" teenagers, enjoy working with them, be firm but fair, and be a great teacher and motivator. It sounded like we were looking for a scout master. Mary and I both thought of Gregg Morrow, the scoutmaster in our local area. He was super with young people. They all loved him. He was also honest, intelligent, hard-working, and savvy with technology. The problem was, Gregg had a good job with 3M, and we were sure he wouldn't be interested in the job. So we used him as our ideal persona in our search for a general manager.

A few months later, we still hadn't found anyone who measured up to Gregg, so I decided to visit him at his office. He listened to my story, smiled, and thanked me for thinking of him. And then he told me no.

A year later we had five stores that were all doing well and 60 employees. I needed a general manager now more than ever, so I went back to visit Gregg. He had watched our progress during the past year and was intrigued with our growth. He decided he wasn't going to change the world from his cubicle at 3M. He wanted to have more influence on young people and the community, and our position was now a good fit for him. Gregg learned the business quickly and took our company from five to more than 60 stores. He was a phenomenal partner for eight years until we sold the company.

Just like our experience with Gregg Morrow, the entrepreneurs we interviewed choose team members primarily based on character. Since many of them run smaller companies, they can't afford to have noxious people in their organization. They tend to look for decent people first and skills second. When you only have five or six people in your company, you can't bury a difficult person deep in a corporate structure. So quality of character has to be a major emphasis when finding team members. Figure 5–2 on page 72 depicts the hiring strategy of many of the entrepreneurs we interviewed.

This simple strategy is not as sophisticated as the ones preached by many academics and human resources experts, but it seems to work well for the entrepreneurs we interviewed across the country. First and foremost, never select team members from Quadrants 1 or 3. You just can't afford the disruption of difficult people in a smaller company. Second, find team members in Quadrant 2 when significant training and experience are not critical. In other words, these roles (store manager, customer support, project management, purchasing, etc.) can be learned quickly by motivated people. Third, choose from Quadrant 4 when substantial education, skills, and expertise are required (engineer, mechanic, graphic designer, architect, etc.). But character is

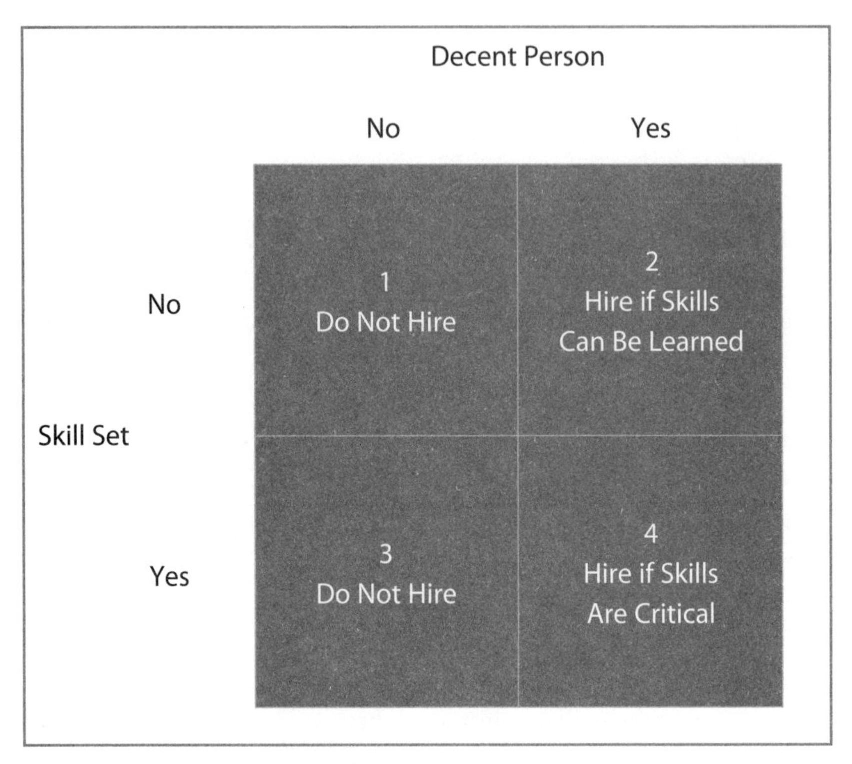

Figure 5–2: **Hiring Decent People**

the primary standard. While everyone's definition of a "decent person" is a bit different, it generally includes these qualities:

- Doesn't lie, cheat, or steal
- Has a strong work ethic
- Is willing to do all the jobs
- Works well in groups
- Keeps ego in check
- Respects people's experience
- Is comfortable with differing opinions

Most important, your team members should be passionate about your purpose, share your values, and fit the culture you are trying to create. Nothing is more exciting than like-minded people enjoying the entrepreneurial experience together. And a highly motivated team with a common purpose will always go farther and faster than any individual working alone. Geese have known this for thousands of years, and we learned it on our bike ride across America. On the other hand, disruptive people take a lot of energy to manage and can drain passion from an organization. So the best hiring strategy for an exciting company is purpose first, character second, and skills third.

The entrepreneurs we interviewed find their team members in a variety of ways. For example, Allen Lim brought in friends he had known for years who had the critical skills his company needed. Steve Sullivan finds partners who love the outdoors and regularly use his products. Justin Gold hires interns from the local university and then keeps the best ones after working with them for several months. And as you would expect, many of the entrepreneurs we met partner with their family members, whom they already know well. Several people even rely on their faith and pray for the right team members. Here's one story we heard.

Bette Hoover and Stan Cole

Bette and Stan are newlyweds. They are also in their late eighties. Bette owns the Hoover Roundup Motel in Walden, Colorado. She purchased the motel from her family estate after her father died, but she and Stan cannot do all the repairs and maintenance needed on the building. Since Walden is located at 8,100 feet elevation with a population of 590, there aren't a lot of people around to help. So Bette started to pray. One day a man named Mick rode into town on his horse, Hawkeye. He had ridden 7,000 miles across America, and his daughter convinced him it was time to find a place to settle down. Stan describes their first encounter:

> *One day a guy come riding in here on a horse. He was hair from here to there. Bette was talking to him, and he wanted a place to stay. He just rode 100 miles on that horse. I saw this developing and kept going, 'No, no, no.' But Bette liked his eyes. So collateral was his chaps, rifle, and Hawkeye his horse, and we gave him a place to stay.*

The first thing Stan wanted to know was whether there was a person under all that hair. He went to the barbershop and asked the price of a haircut. Matt, the barber, told him $15. Stan said, "That's a fair price, but not for what I'm going to bring you." Stan gave him $25 and went to get Mick. He told Matt, "Cut until you find somebody under there." Afterward, the first thing Mick said was that his neck was really cold.

Mick worked at the motel for several weeks and did all the needed repairs. He cleaned up the mess behind the motel and kept his horse back there. When word got out about his skills, a local contractor hired him and gave him a nice salary. Mick was still living at the Roundup Motel a year later when we visited Walden. He continues to help Bette and Stan with anything that needs to be done. Here is how Stan feels about Mick now:

> *He was a godsend. He has done so much for this place to help us. We just can't enumerate the kinds of things he is capable of. There isn't anything the guy can't do. He is a handyman deluxe. He has a sixth sense about things. He's just a really good guy.*

The simple process of looking for decent people first and skills second yields high dividends. Many of the entrepreneurs we met have kept their core team together for 10, 15, or 20 years, but Richard Macher holds the record. He is the owner of Macado's, a lively bar and restaurant chain with 20 locations in small towns around the Southeast. Richard hires great people and lets them participate in the growth and development of the business:

> *I have hired everyone right out of high school, and they have stuck with me ever since. My office staff has been with me for more than a hundred years combined: one 37 years, one 35 years, one 25 years, and one 18 years. I have four district managers and an operations guy who have 123 years here together. I give them lots of responsibility. Self-actualization is my number-one thing. People gotta feel like they're important and engaged.*

Building a strong team is not an easy task. Mountains of books have been written on the topic. In reality, things don't always work out the way you want. You learn a lot by trial and error. Finding decent people who share your purpose, and letting them participate fully in the entrepreneurial process, goes a long way toward building an exciting and successful organization.

Building Strategic Partnerships

We had several core competencies in our frozen foods business. We created healthy products that tasted great. We successfully marketed our products through wholesale and retail channels. We gave phenomenal customer service. We were excellent planners and executors. And we ran an extremely efficient operation with no debt. However, we were not very good at designing our retail spaces, making our cabinetry, constructing our stores, manufacturing our product, or sourcing and maintaining our equipment. So we cultivated long-term partnerships with people and companies that did these things far better than we could. We stuck with our core competencies and relied on them for their expertise, essentially creating a machine that hummed along at top speed.

We stayed with the same architect, cabinetmaker, contractor, manufacturer, and equipment supplier for nearly ten years. Thus we never wasted any time shopping around for new partners. So how did we keep from being taken advantage of? We sat down with each partner and said: "We really like your work and would like to stay with you as we scale our business. What we need is fair pricing that we can always count on." Then we agreed to "cost plus" pricing, set profit margins, fixed fees per case, etc. We built a team that was able to move quickly, and we never had to worry about overpaying for anything. These were remarkable win-win partnerships.

We saw this same phenomenon as we interviewed entrepreneurs across the country. Nearly all of them have strong strategic partners they have relied on for years. They continue to use the same suppliers, distributors, designers, accountants, and service providers. These mutually beneficial relationships allow them to do what they do well, while meeting critical business needs through others. Here is a great example of the way strategic partnerships can build a company.

Dan and Suzanne Marino

> *I was sitting in the back seat of our '73 Blazer. My mom's up in front, and I tap her on the shoulder and say, 'When I get out of school, I am moving to Jackson Hole.' I never said another word about it. I graduated from school, the next day packed up my 1966 Mustang, and she says, 'Where on earth are you going?' I say, 'I told you four years ago I am going to Jackson Hole.' And I have been here ever since.*

Dan moved to Jackson Hole, Wyoming, right after high school because he loved the city, skiing, and being outdoors. There was no way he was going to sit at a desk all day. Over the next decade he taught skiing lessons, cleaned diesel engines, worked in restaurants, and eventually built a successful pressure washing company.

Dan grew up in a family of four boys, and growing boys are always hungry. "We weren't by any stretch of the imagination a wealthy family," he says, "so we needed to supply some of our own goods." So Dan hunted for pheasants, ducks, geese, deer, and elk. He would go out early in the morning before school and then go out again afterward. If he harvested a bird or an animal, he would clean it, process it, and take good care of the meat. If he wasn't successful, he didn't mind because he loved hiking in the woods and getting a chance to connect with the world. While he worked in restaurants in Jackson Hole, he continued to refine the skills he had learned early on: he cut sirloins, rib eyes, and fillets and made hamburgers.

Suzanne also fell in love with Jackson Hole. While attending college in California, she visited some friends there who were playing in a band. They took her fishing, and she said, "I'm moving here." When she graduated from college, she moved to Jackson Hole, and a year later she bought a downtown restaurant called the Cadillac Grille and ran it for a number of years. When Dan sold his pressure washing business, they bought the Jackson Hole Buffalo Meat Company. At the time, the company processed game, but it was mostly a cold storage facility. Dan was excited to use his game processing skills to build a much bigger and more ambitious business.

The Jackson Hole Buffalo Meat Company is now a national brand. Dan and Suzanne process 100 percent natural, free-range–raised buffalo and elk meat that is lower in fat and higher in protein, iron, and other vitamins and minerals than beef. They make steaks, roasts, burgers, sausages, salami, and jerky. They package and label their own products and then ship them across the country. Early on they were featured on a show called *Food Finds* on the Food Network, which "was an epic boon" for the company. Since then, Dan and Suzanne have moved the business to an attractive storefront and added a number of gift products unique to Jackson Hole: sauces, spices, syrups, jams, glassware, cutlery, and a variety of gift packs. Approximately half of their business comes from local customers, and the other half comes from customers across the United States who order on the company website.

Strategic partnerships have been a huge part of Dan and Suzanne's success. Because Dan taught ski lessons for a number of years and Suzanne ran a popular restaurant, they know everybody. All their elk and buffalo meat comes from local ranchers. The gifts they sell are made by local vendors and artists, which makes their products unique. They also have great relationships with local hotels, banks, caterers, and wedding planners. These businesses regularly buy gift packs from Dan and Suzanne for their own customers. Equally impressive are the relationships Dan and Suzanne have developed with clubs and nonprofits in the area. They support the Jaycees (the United States Junior Chamber), the Lions Club, the local Elks lodge, and other organizations. Their support for these groups creates goodwill for their business in the community that they love. Dan believes all these relationships are win-win partnerships that benefit all parties involved:

> *There are only a limited number of suppliers in our industry, so it's critical that we develop strong relationships with the ranchers and slaughterhouses. These people are not just my business partners, they are my friends. If the supply ever gets short, they sell to me, so I am always secure. . . . On the customer side, we sell to a number of businesses that give our products to their customers. So the local ranchers supply us and we supply local businesses. It is really important to us*

to build local partnerships. Our company wouldn't be what it is today without these relationships.

REFLECTION

Assessing Your Team Needs

Successful entrepreneurs build a supporting cast of people around them in three ways: First, they develop a brain trust of mentors who advise them for free. Second, they find passionate team members who believe in their cause. And third, they create strategic partnerships that facilitate the growth of their business. It's all about relationships: The more win-win affiliations you create, the more successful you will be—plain and simple! Below is an assessment activity that will help you determine what types of mentors, team members, and partners you will need to grow your business.

In the left-hand column below are descriptions of skills that are often needed in organizations. In the second column, evaluate how important each skill is to the overall success of your venture. In the third column, indicate how strongly you possess that skill. This will help you determine what you need in your company, what you have personally, and where you need mentors and team members to fill in the gaps.

Key

How Important?	Your Strength?
1 = seldom needed	1 = fairly weak
2 = occasionally needed	2 = moderate
3 = critical to success	3 = very strong

Company Leadership	How Important?	Your Strength?
Business Planning: defining a clear company purpose; understanding the planning process; developing short and long-term objectives; and creating annual execution plans	1 2 3	1 2 3
Product Development: generating new product and service ideas based on intimate knowledge of customers; determining ideas that should be prototyped and tested in the market	1 2 3	1 2 3
Communication: possessing excellent oral, written, and presentation skills; convincingly communicating the company purpose, strategy, and values to team members, investors, and company partners	1 2 3	1 2 3
Creating Partnerships: identifying mentors and advisors to help with the business; creating win-win strategic partnerships with other companies	1 2 3	1 2 3

Team Building	How Important?	Your Strength?
Recruiting and Hiring: identifying the kinds of team members needed in the venture; attracting potential partners; enticing key individuals to join the organization	1 2 3	1 2 3
Training and Development: identifying training needs for various roles in the company; designing effective training programs to develop required skill sets	1 2 3	1 2 3

Team Building	How Important?	Your Strength?
Managing Performance: understanding the goal-setting process; acquiring buy-in from team members; providing ongoing feedback through effective coaching; managing conflict when it arises	1 2 3	1 2 3
Problem Solving: anticipating problems that may arise and creating plans to avoid them; analyzing and solving problems that do arise in the organization	1 2 3	1 2 3

Sales and Marketing	How Important?	Your Strength?
Product Pricing: calculating competitive pricing, product margins, and break-even analysis; pricing products in the market based on existing price structure	1 2 3	1 2 3
Marketing Strategy: planning advertising, promotions, and sales campaigns; establishing channels of distribution; recruiting a strong sales force or networks of distributors	1 2 3	1 2 3
Ecommerce: maintaining an appealing website; building a social media presence; creating sales and marketing programs on the internet; optimizing search rankings; transacting business online	1 2 3	1 2 3
Customer Service: determining customer needs and preferences; creating a system to deliver excellent service; training and managing a superb customer service team	1 2 3	1 2 3

Production and Operations	How Important?	Your Strength?
Purchasing: identifying multiple suppliers of materials and goods; negotiating attractive purchasing contracts; receiving and managing flow of materials and goods into inventory	1 2 3	1 2 3
Manufacturing: possessing knowledge of manufacturing planning; managing production within time constraints, quality requirements, and budget; establishing effective inventory and quality controls	1 2 3	1 2 3
Distribution: setting up and managing the flow of products from production through channels of distribution to customers; managing margins along the supply chain	1 2 3	1 2 3
Information Technology: understanding various information systems required for company growth; sourcing and selecting appropriate software and hardware	1 2 3	1 2 3

Accounting and Finance	How Important?	Your Strength?
Capital Budgeting: acquiring initial startup funds; forecasting future funding needs; preparing capital budgets; and allocating expenditures	1 2 3	1 2 3
Accounting: using appropriate bookkeeping systems; preparing income statements, balance sheets, and break-even analysis; managing cash flow, payables, receivables, and bank relations	1 2 3	1 2 3

Accounting and Finance	How Important?	Your Strength?
Taxes: complying with state and federal reporting requirements; being familiar with compensation regulations and payroll tax; understanding tax consequences of bonus and benefit plans	1 2 3	1 2 3
Credit and Collections: developing credit policies, screening criteria, and collection practices; implementing a system for effectively acquiring funds owed to the company	1 2 3	1 2 3

Legal Issues	How Important?	Your Strength?
Organization: understanding various forms of organizing a company, including partnerships and corporations; understanding rights, obligations, and roles of directors, officers, and shareholders	1 2 3	1 2 3
Contracts: understanding various types of government and commercial contracts; understanding leasing, licensing, franchising, and other agreements	1 2 3	1 2 3
Intellectual Property: understanding patents, trademarks, copyrights, and trade secrets; knowing how to manage intellectual property and keep it protected	1 2 3	1 2 3
Real Estate: understanding options for physical facilities and the advantages of each; understanding the agreements necessary for renting, leasing, purchasing, or selling property	1 2 3	1 2 3

Each skill you rated a 3 in the second column is a skill that needs to be filled within your organization. If you also gave the skill a 3 in the third column, that is something you can do yourself. However, skills you rated a 3 in the second column but scored a 1 or 2 in the third column need to be filled by other people who are experts at that particular skill. At first you can meet these needs with mentors and advisors because you won't have a lot of cash. As your business grows, you can fill these roles with full-time team members and strategic partners. Good luck building your supporting cast.

CHAPTER

6

Maximize All Available Resources

"I think you have to challenge every dollar you are about to spend. You don't need a fancy sign. You don't need fancy cubicles. Just look for alternatives. Never assume there is one way. If you're about to purchase something, pause for a moment and say, 'How else can I do this?'"

—Mark Soderberg, CEO of Boa Technology

One of the questions people ask me about our bike trip across America is, "How much did it cost?" They think the number will be pretty big: four people, a 33-foot motorhome, food, equipment, supplies, etc. When I tell them "almost nothing," they are very surprised, until I explain.

I was sitting in my office one day at Utah State University when Spencer Bailey, the president of our entrepreneurship club, came to see me. He is a cycling enthusiast and knew about our plans to ride across the country to interview entrepreneurs.

"Hey, Mike," he said, "your ride across America is a perfect Kickstarter campaign."

"I don't think so, Spencer. We don't have a product or a slick new technology," I replied.

"That doesn't matter. You are helping people start their own businesses, and we can create some great reward packages for your backers."

The more we talked, the more I thought Spencer might be right. At least I was willing to give it a try. It would be a great story to tell our students if it worked. So Spencer agreed to help with the campaign. We created a video about how technology is eliminating jobs and how we were going to help redefine the American Dream. We offered backers a variety of packages that included stickers, T-shirts, hoodies, a copy of the book, and opportunities to join us on our ride. We also created some packages for corporate sponsors. The result: We raised $28,455 in 30 days. While a lot of the money came from the corporate sponsors we recruited, Kickstarter gave the project credibility and a format for the donations.

The Kickstarter fund paid all our basic expenses, but one of the biggest costs was the motorhome. Although we may not use this option next time, it saved us thousands of dollars. It costs about $8,000 per month to rent a 33-foot motorhome. I spoke with a few dealers around town, and they suggested I buy one instead and then sell it when we returned. They were confident I could sell it for close to its purchase price if it had low mileage and was in good condition. So I bought a motorhome. It gave us a place to sleep, which reduced our lodging expenses, and Sinclair Oil paid for most of our gas. Although we had our debacle on White Bird Hill and were out of our league with RV care and maintenance, our insurance company paid 100 percent of the repairs. In the aftermath, the drive train, muffler, tailpipe, and batteries were brand-new. I sold the bus the following spring for close to what I paid for it, so our total cost wound up being far less than $8,000 per month.

Effectiveness and Efficiency

As an entrepreneur and business consultant, I have learned there are always ways to produce big-time results with small means, as we did with our bike ride across America. I start each project by focusing on two important concepts: effectiveness and efficiency. Effectiveness is achieving critical objectives for growing your business; efficiency is doing it with as few resources as possible. Here is a simple analogy to illustrate these two concepts. Suppose you have a bee buzzing around your kitchen that is driving you crazy. Your objective is to get rid of it (effectiveness). One solution is to grab a sledgehammer from the garage and start swinging away. While this approach will eventually kill the bee, it takes a lot of energy and will do serious damage to your kitchen. The more common solution is to start chasing the bee around your house with a fly swatter, which will also kill the bee, but still requires some effort on your part. A third solution is to simply open a door and let the bee fly away. While all three solutions are *effective* in getting rid of the bee, the third is by far the most *efficient*. It requires less time and fewer resources.

Applying this analogy to business, the sledgehammer solution is extravagant and excessive. It's what big corporations and governments often do. The fly swatter solution is the status quo. It is what most companies do. Opening doors is what entrepreneurs do. It's not because they are geniuses—it's because they generally lack funding and have to use other means to get things done. You can be very creative when you have to be, and there are lots of ways to open doors while building a business. Here are some examples from the frozen dessert company we built and sold.

One of our biggest challenges was creating our own proprietary line of nonfat, low-calorie products that tasted great. We needed a research lab to do this, and they are very expensive. Building our own was the sledgehammer solution. Renting one was the fly-swatter option. Since we had limited funds, we needed to open a door. What we did was partner with a local university that had a state-of-the-art dairy lab. We let graduate students assist as interns on the project and paid the university a small monthly fee to use the lab. In the end, our cost to create 30 excellent flavors was far below the industry standard.

Another challenge was producing our products. The sledgehammer solution was to build a multimillion-dollar plant. The fly-swatter solution was to rent space in an existing facility. What we did was partner with a large grocery chain that had just built a state-of-the-art ice cream plant. They produced our products for a set fee per gallon above their cost and then allowed us to sell our products in their grocery stores. It was a win-win strategic partnership.

The last example involved changing our name in a sales region. We started the company in Utah and had great success. As we expanded out of the state, we were not able to secure a federal trademark for our original brand. We finally obtained a new federal trademark that we used to expand outside Utah, and then we decided to go back and change our name in the original region to match. We were concerned our sales might drop if customers thought we were a new business with new owners. So at first we got bids for a typical media campaign to explain our name change that included radio, television, and print ads. It was a very expensive sledgehammer solution. Then we had an idea. Rather than getting a 1 to 2 percent response rate from expensive advertising, why not give away free product in our stores to our existing customers and everyone else who showed up? So we put banners on all our stores that said "FREE YOGURT FRIDAY NIGHT" and told all our customers about the event and our new name. We ended up feeding thousands of people, and the media showed up to cover the frenzy for free. A local television station actually broadcast part of their nightly newscast from one of our stores. As a result, our name change was communicated in a positive way and our sales went up. We ended up doing the promotion every time we opened a new store. It was a very effective low-cost strategy for grand openings.

Our Resourceful Entrepreneurs

The entrepreneurs we met on our bike ride, and others I have interviewed over the past 20 years, are masters of efficiency. They create new ventures from practically nothing, get more from less along the way, and keep costs below industry standards. They have a real knack for finding and using a host of resources other than money: They find free advisors, acquire used equipment, defer compensation, negotiate excellent terms, partner with their customers, and use someone else's building rather than buy one. They think resources first and cash second. The strategy is to create a low-cost prototype, prove that it works, and then grow with cash flow. You have seen this approach used by entrepreneurs you have met in previous chapters. Omer Orian developed a large customer base by operating his first Off the Waffle store out of his home. Mary DeLima got her first three lesson horses for DeLima Stables from people whose children and grandchildren had outgrown their horses. And Joanne McCall sold her first public relations contract to her current employer before spending a lot of time and resources launching the McCall Media Group. Here are some more detailed stories about maximizing resources from our excellent role models.

Justin Gold

Justin was making the best nut butters on the planet with a food processor in his home kitchen. When he decided to scale up his business, he talked with several large peanut butter manufacturers. He told them what he wanted to do: add honey, maple syrup, and other ingredients. They said it couldn't be done. They told him their large industrial grinders with rotating plates would burn out if they added things like honey and syrup. He thought it was funny that he could do it in a "rinky-dink food processor" in his kitchen, but they couldn't do it in their multimillion-dollar plants:

> *So instead of buying a $50,000 piece of equipment that everybody else had, I tried to think in terms of food processing. I went out and found the oldest industrial food processors I could find that were way cheaper than a peanut butter mill and got them to work. It's a bunch of machines that do not belong together. The end result is the perfect peanut butter, and it has to do with being resourceful. It's amazing how creative you can get when you have to be. Thinking outside the box gave us a completely unique product that our competitors can't mimic. . . . With everything our company has done, I'm constantly making sure we are not overspending.*

Amy Gardner

Amy, founder of Scarpa, tells a similar story about being resourceful when you have limited funding. Amy has to pay her suppliers to continue getting shoes. If her accounts are not paid up, she can't acquire inventory for each new season. During the recession of 2009, her sales were down between 30 and 50 percent most months. With funding nearly impossible to obtain, she turned to her customers for help. She offered them a 25 percent discount if they would buy a $10,000 gift certificate, and a 20 percent discount for a $5,000 gift certificate. Two customers wrote checks for $10,000 and ten wrote checks for $5,000.

Amy's resourcefulness raised $70,000, and her business continued to improve over the next few years. By the summer of 2013, her sales were up 40 percent from the previous year. Her unconventional strategy worked because she has a loyal group of high-end customers who love both her products and the way they are treated in her store.

Allen Lim

Allen and his partners at Skratch Labs were building their company with cash flow. They had to get big-time results without spending a lot of money. To reach their audience, they needed to show up at sporting events like marathons, 10Ks, triathlons, bicycle races, and so on. Without funding, they had to get creative:

> *What we decided to do was invest in an abandoned funnel cake truck. It was a 20-foot trailer that was at an old carnival. We converted it into a full kitchen. We started towing it around the country cooking real food for people while at the same time obtaining attention for our sports drink. The money we made cooking paid for our way to these events. It was really effective! At the end of our first year, our total marketing expense was about $800 because we made up that difference by selling burritos. Literally! We just took the carnival on the road.*

Here is another great example of how Allen and his team got enormous results with very little money. They wanted to sponsor the AMGEN Tour of California, the biggest bicycle race in the country, but they didn't have the $250,000 required to get into the event. With their backgrounds in cycling, they knew that every race had a neutral support vehicle that provided mechanical aid to any cyclist who needed it. They thought, "Why not use a neutral human support vehicle to provide food and drinks to the riders?" They pitched the idea to the AMGEN organizers, who thought it was phenomenal. Skratch Labs became the neutral food and drink support sponsor for all the teams and riders without paying the large sponsorship fee, and they got remarkable publicity with their target audience:

> *We ended up getting a motorcycle and a car embedded in the race with our logo and branding on them. We were making like 800 little sushi rice cakes each day as well as cookies and real food. Instead of processed energy bars, they got this fresh food from scratch every day. They also got our all-natural sports drink, and we were a big hit with the riders. For us, it was a creative way to get big-time marketing access by working for it rather than paying for it. I think I was on the news something like 11 times that week, in part because we had a real story to tell.*

Jeff Wester

Jeff had a good friend whose family was in the horseshoeing business. His friend's father had a shop with an old coal forge with a hand-cranked blower. Jeff and his buddy would go out there for hours and make things out of metal. One day his friend told him, "Jeff, God made you to be a blacksmith." Jeff was actually intrigued by the idea. He knew that in frontier days the blacksmith shop was the center of town, where the blacksmith made the tools for all the other craftsmen. Jeff wondered if an old-fashioned blacksmith shop could still be viable in a small town.

Jeff went on to earn a degree in mechanical and manufacturing engineering at the Oregon Institute of Technology. When he graduated, all the jobs were in the aerospace industry. All of his fellow graduates were taking jobs with Boeing, Hughes, and McDonnell Douglas and moving to Seattle, San Francisco, and Los Angeles. Jeff didn't want to work for a big company, and he didn't want to live in a big city.

So he moved to Sisters, Oregon, and started a horseshoeing business. He operated his small business in everything from a tent to the back of his house. In 1989, he decided he was ready to build his broader blacksmith business—Ponderosa Forge and Ironworks. He had had two successful years working with contractors and builders and knew the concept would work. He now needed his own shop. Since money was not available without significant collateral, which he didn't have, he had to find a creative solution:

> *There was this old guy named Joe Fought who owned Fought Steel in Portland. He started out as a blacksmith himself back in the 1920s. Anyone who wanted to start a business could go to this old guy, and if he liked your plan, he would give you whatever money you wanted at 12 percent. He owned this lot and said, 'You figure out what you want to build, and when you need money, call me. I will send you the money and a promissory note. When you get your shop built and you are working in it, we will add up all the promissory notes and make a little contract.' So that's how I got started.*

In addition to securing financing from Fought, Jeff found great used equipment at auctions. A lot of mills were going out of business at the time, and they all had blacksmith shops, welding shops, and machine shops. Jeff got super deals at auction prices. When he analyzed all his costs, he realized he could pay off his loan from Fought just by shoeing horses, so he put some hitching rails in front of his shop. If nothing more happened, he would eventually own a fully furnished blacksmith shop. So it was not a big risk.

Today, Jeff has a group of excellent blacksmiths working in the business. They do machining, welding, and general repair, just like blacksmith shops did more than 100 years ago. They also make 130 products they sell from their showroom and online: towel rings, cabinet knobs, door handles, fireplace tools, railings, brackets, lights, and chandeliers. Jeff is living his dream. He owns an old-fashioned blacksmith shop, where, as his website puts it, "the sound of hammers and the roar of fire break the silence of a small western town."

Chris Washburn

Chris believes that bicycle manufacturers may end up pricing themselves right out of the market. If the price tag on lightweight carbon fiber bikes continues to climb, a large portion of the population may not be able to afford them. Chris loves biking and is passionate about solving this problem.

After earning an MBA and a law degree, Chris worked for Lee Iacocca, who was building an electric vehicle company. A few years later he worked for a company that was designing and building electric bicycles for the military. He was commuting from Utah to Washignton, D.C. weekly. After missing too many of his kids' soccer and baseball games, he was done with traveling. That's when he started Fezzari Bicycles.

Chris wrote a business plan and shopped it around for financing. An investor was willing to give him $1 million for equity in the company. On his way to the investor's office to sign the papers, Chris called his wife, and she asked, "How do you feel about it?" Chris said, "It doesn't feel exactly right for some reason." His wife replied, "Well, don't do it." So he backed out of the deal and funded the company with personal savings and a couple of short-term bank loans.

Initially, Chris built a good-quality but lower-cost bike for Costco. Though his company was vulnerable to the whims of one large customer, this contract produced cash flow and allowed him to further develop his product line and business model. Of these early days, Chris says:

> *We ran a very tight ship and were profitable from day one. A lot of times we couldn't get something done, so we would do it ourselves, whether it was designing ads, programming, photo shooting, or engineering. It was a lot of hard work, but as a startup company you don't have much money you can throw around. I think it is best just to tell your story and be honest, as opposed to trying to do some exotic spin and pay a lot of money to have it done.*

Three words summarize the Fezzari story: custom, quality, direct. First, they customize every bike for every customer, regardless of the price of the bike. They collect your height, weight, inseam, arm length, torso length, and shoulder width, and then they build your bike from the ground up. With a 23-point setup process, every bike is a perfect fit. And when your bike fits better, you feel better, and you ride it more.

Next, Fezzari is fanatical about quality. They use all the same materials and components as other high-end bike manufacturers, but they sell their bikes for 30 to 40 percent less. This means their Catania road bike ($979) is comparable to other $1,500 bikes. On the high end, their CR5 ($5,199) is comparable to an $8,500 bike. It was voted one of the top seven road bikes of 2014 by *Outside* magazine.

Finally, the company's direct-selling model saves customers hundreds and even thousands of dollars. While most bikes go from the manufacturer to a distributor to a retail bike shop, Fezzari bikes are sold directly to you. You visit their online showroom, select your bike, provide your measurements, and they build your bike and mail it to you. You get a fantastic bike with a perfect fit for a remarkable price.

Fezzari now sells thousands of bikes all over the world. According to Chris, they have two types of customers. The first type does a ton of research and spends an hour on the phone with a sales associate. After these people buy a bike, the second type of customer shows up. These customers are referrals from the first type of buyer, who see their bike and love it. More than 60 percent of Fezzari buyers are repeat customers or referrals. So the business model is working: Their success comes from a passion to solve a pricing problem, a very lean operation, and a low-cost delivery system.

Capital-Intensive Industries

When I speak to audiences, I often get the following comment: "Your low-cost startup model is great for service companies, but it won't work in capital-intensive industries like mine." I explain that maximizing all available resources is a sound business strategy in any industry. There are always things you can do. It's a matter of asking the question: "How do we get the exact same result (effectiveness) with the lowest possible cost (efficiency)?" Then I tell them stories of entrepreneurs I have interviewed in capital-intensive industries who started their companies with very little funding. You have already learned how Dave Twombly financed his garbage company primarily with equipment leases. From his experience in the industry, he knew that each truck he put on the road could earn enough revenue to pay all the associated costs plus the lease payment and still make money. Here are a few more examples.

Robin Petgrave

Robin had a recurring dream as a young man in which he was a superhero who had figured out a remarkable secret: If he dove at the ground with his arms back and had total faith, he would defy gravity and start to fly. The reason no one else had figured this out was because they always flinched. If you flinch, you become subject to the laws of gravity and crash. "Sometimes I'd get so close to the ground my skin was almost touching," Robin says. "But if I had total faith and didn't flinch, I would start to fly." Of course, Robin never tried this in real life; it was just a dream. "But almost every night, I'd be flying around saving people and doing this Superman stuff," he says. "In the morning I was like, 'Man! That was cool.'"

One day Robin took a helicopter ride and met the young pilot. He assumed the man had learned to fly in the military. When he found out the pilot had simply taken lessons and gotten his license, he knew what he wanted to do. After obtaining his license, he went to work for a flight training school. One day he had an argument with his boss. Robin felt the helicopter he was flying needed maintenance, but his boss disagreed and grounded him for four days. Unable to fly and with $300 to his name, he knew he had to do something.

Robin visited a company that leased helicopters out of the Torrance Airport. They told him they would lease him one for a $6,000 deposit and a commitment to fly 80 hours a month. If he didn't use the 80 hours each month, he would have to pay for them anyway. Robin explained that he only had $300 and somehow persuaded them to waive the deposit and the 80-hour monthly minimum. Just like that, he was in business! He found a handful of students and charged them 50 percent more per hour than he was paying for the helicopter. This was for the flight time only; he also charged them an hourly fee for the lessons. Robin billed $18,000 his first month. Before long, he was leasing additional helicopters and hiring pilots. Then he started buying helicopters. Today, Celebrity Helicopters, based in Compton, California, does training, tours, charter flights, and aerial filming for the entertainment industry. Robin has even been a helicopter pilot in several movies. He no longer has his dream of flying as a superhero. He is living his dream in real life.

Jon Huntsman Sr.

Jon graduated from the Wharton School in 1959 and took a job selling eggs in Los Angeles. According to Jon, it "was about as unglamorous a job as a Wharton graduate has ever taken." The company, Olson Brothers, owned major ranches and egg production plants around the western United States. When Jon hired on, he was part of a team that was developing a new plastic egg carton to replace the traditional pulp carton. During this time, the company merged with Dow Chemical and created a 50/50 joint venture. Jon eventually became the president of the joint venture, and the company did extremely well under his leadership.

One year for Christmas, Jon received a book from the president of Dow Chemical entitled *The Dow Story*. It told how Herbert Dow decided he no longer wanted to work for anyone else, so he started his own company in a shack adjacent to his home. Jon thought, "If Mr. Dow can go out and start his own company, I would like to do likewise." So Jon left Dow Chemical and started several companies of his own, including the Huntsman Container Corp., the company that pioneered the plastic clamshell Big Mac container for McDonald's. Jon later sold this business to the Keyes Fiber Company.

After taking a three-year break to serve on a mission for his church, Jon decided he wanted to start a new business in the petrochemical industry. At the time, many products made of paper, wood, metal, and glass were being converted to plastic, so he knew there was a bright future in the industry. Here is how he pulled off an unbelievable acquisition of his first plant with limited personal funding:

I began negotiating with Shell Oil Company to buy their polystyrene plant in Belpre, Ohio. They couldn't conceive an individual paying $42 million for a single manufacturing plant. When I told them I would put up $500,000 in equity, they just about tossed me out of their office. But I was able to string together the most unique financing arrangement ever concocted. I persuaded Shell to take back a $12 million note that I would pay off over the next ten years. I then met with ARCO and told them I'd buy 150 million pounds of styrene monomer from them each year for 13 years—the raw material for polystyrene—if they would loan me $10 million upfront. They finally agreed to do it over the objections of many of their senior officers. With my $500,000, the $12 million note from Shell, and the $10 million loan from ARCO, I was able to persuade one of my former classmates at Wharton, who was now the executive vice president of Union Bank in Los Angeles, to loan me the remaining $20 million. It was literally hooked together with chewing gum and bailing wire.

So Jon bought a $42 million plant for $500,000 of personal funds, which equaled 1.2 percent of the total purchase price. He operated this plant according to three guiding principles that he would repeat again and again in every plant he purchased: create a quality product, run the plant at maximum capacity, and operate it very efficiently. Today, Huntsman Corporation is a multibillion-dollar company with plants all over the world.

Planning to Maximize Resources

Successful business builders don't just start off lean but continue to orchestrate marvelous efficiencies while growing their business. This sharp eye for "creating more from less" offers a tremendous competitive advantage. Being the low-cost operator in an industry allows you to: 1) maintain market prices and reap larger margins than your competitors or 2) lower your prices and quickly pick up market share. So, identifying and maximizing resources needs to be an ongoing part of your strategy. Having worked with hundreds of entrepreneurs, I have put together a simple yet effective planning process that keeps you focused on your purpose and makes resource maximization a priority.

Step 1: Revisit Your "Why"

Revisiting your "why" reminds you of your purpose for building your company in the first place. If you don't do this often, it's easy to stray from your firm foundation. In *Start with Why*, Simon Sinek skillfully argues that many large corporations have lost their way—Walmart, Starbucks, Dell—and then struggled to get back to their purpose. Other companies, like Southwest Airlines, have kept their original engaging purpose from day one. While your purpose is relatively stable over long periods of time, it can change. Recall how Gail and Will Williams started Idaho Sewing for Sports to create a new life for their family in a beautiful location. As the company stabilized, their purpose shifted to creating jobs for people who are struggling. The important point is you always need to know why you are doing what you are doing.

Step 2: Define Your "What"

Your "what" defines the type of company you are going to build within your "why." It is a vision of what you want your company to be in two to three years. Just like an architect creates a beautiful rendering of a building to be constructed, you need to create an image of the company you will build. This "what" should include the products you will create, the markets you will serve, the teammates you will hire, the customers you will acquire, the revenue you will achieve, the margins you will obtain, and so on. While your "why" remains fairly constant over time, your "what" can change every few years. For example, Apple has changed its "what" a number of times, from computers to music devices to phones and watches, but it has always stayed within the "why" of innovative technology that makes our lives better.

Step 3: Plan Your "How"

Now it is time to define the "how," or the specific objectives you must achieve in the short run to approximate the vision you have created in your "what." I call this a one-year execution plan. These are the big rocks you have to move this year to achieve the two- to three-year vision you have defined for your company. I find that four to six major goals or initiatives are about right for a given year.

These need to be specific milestones, like increasing sales by 30 percent, adding three new products, opening two additional locations, and so on. After defining these key outcomes (effectiveness), you need to spend at least as much time planning how you will achieve these results with minimal resources (efficiency). This is the task most companies gloss over, but if you spend as much time deciding how you will efficiently achieve your goals as you do on setting them, you will become very good at maximizing resources. It will become a habit. Remember, there are always ways to produce big results with small means, which is critical to an entrepreneur's long-term success and sustainability.

REFLECTION

Strategies for Efficiency

In summary, here is a list of 14 valuable strategies I have seen successful entrepreneurs use over the years to launch and grow their companies with minimal costs. Study this list carefully and decide which of these you can use in your new enterprise.

1. Mentors and Advisors

In Chapter 5, you learned how to build a brain trust of mentors and advisors. Use this group as much as you can for advice, feedback, and meeting other important contacts.

2. Free Consulting Services

Organizations like SCORE and your local Small Business Development Center (SBDC) offer free consulting and training. SCORE has more than 300 chapters in the United States, and everyone who calls gets an appointment. There are nearly 1,000 SBDCs in the United States that offer free consulting and educational services.

3. Barter or Trade

Bartering—swapping one thing for another—has been an effective way of doing business for centuries. In recent years, bartering has evolved into a sound strategy for finding goods, trading services, conserving cash, moving inventory, and locating excess production capacity. The International Reciprocal Trade Association (IRTA) helps match up companies interested in bartering for goods and services (www.irta.com).

4. Nonmonetary Incentives

Members of your team will often work for equity or deferred payments rather than initial salaries. This will keep costs down during the launch and early growth stages of your business.

5. Supplier Partnerships

The right suppliers can save you a great deal of time and money: They can provide high-quality materials, help with product development, offer on-time delivery, and allow extended payment terms. Obtaining 30 to 90 days of trade credit is the best business loan you can get.

6. Customer Partnerships

Partnering with customers during your launch is an excellent cost-saving strategy. Select a few key customers and offer them deals they cannot refuse: discounted pricing, special packaging, strong support, etc. In exchange, ask for long-term commitments to purchase your products. And whenever possible, get customers to pay early—ideally, even before you deliver their products or services.

7. Outsourcing

Outsourcing is a multibillion-dollar industry. You can find outsource partners to provide just about any product or service. Outsourcing turns what would normally be a fixed cost into a variable cost because you only use the service when you need it.

8. Distributors, Reps, Affiliate Partners

Most industries have distributors, manufacturers' representatives, and affiliate partners who will sell your products through their existing distribution channels, which can be extensive. This is a great way to build sales quickly and conserve cash because you don't pay the partner until your products are sold.

9. Commissioned Sales Force

Use a commission sales program when you are ready to hire team members to sell. This will attract people who really believe in you, your products, and your purpose. It also conserves cash by keeping your fixed costs low.

10. Work Virtually

In this new age of technology, it is possible to work from just about anywhere: from home, in your car, at the airport, or in a hotel room. Thus, it is not necessary to take on the expense of establishing an office when launching your business.

11. Borrow, Rent, Buy Used

Find ways to use other people's resources in addition to your own. Whenever possible, borrow rather than rent; rent rather than buy; and buy used rather than new. Some industries have excellent equipment available for a dime on the dollar. Also, go to bankruptcy sales and auctions.

12. Use Free Software

Free and inexpensive software is plentiful online. Various programs can help you manage your finances, plan your projects, track your customers, and much more. You can also take advantage of free trial periods for most business software. This gives you a chance to use the application for free for 30 days or more to determine if you really need it.

13. Minimize Your Expenses

Keep your personal expenses to a minimum when launching your new venture. This is not the time to buy a new house or a new car or take on personal debt. The longer you can live with minimal expenses, the better off you will be. Likewise, don't take on any ongoing business expenses unless they are absolutely necessary.

14. Sell, Sell, Sell

In startup companies everyone is in sales. All your team members need to talk about your company, promote your products, and assume responsibility for producing revenue. Remember, low costs and early cash flow are critical to success.

CHAPTER
7

Work with Zealous Tenacity

"You see it in their actions; you hear it in their voice. And the same thing that compels them becomes part of their ability to make it compelling to you. You're drawn to it like a moth to a flame. And that enthusiasm becomes the central fuel that propels the project forward. It grows like a series of concentric circles."

—Ric Burns, founder of Steeplechase Films

Marti McMahon was one of the first entrepreneurs I interviewed nearly 20 years ago. I immediately felt her palpable passion and her off-the-charts tenacity. I thought, "Surely she must be an outlier on these two qualities." Marti told me she had three great loves: boats, people, and entertaining. She longed to combine these loves in her own business. Her dream was to own and operate a fleet of yachts that offered gourmet dining during scenic cruises of the San Francisco Harbor. She bought her first boat in Florida and sailed it through the Panama Canal and back to San Francisco with her three young children. They survived a major storm, a month of boat repairs, fights with Mexican customers, food poisoning, and the company of her bedraggled crew. Of this adventure, she says:

> *I had a captain who had been married three times, an alcoholic tutor for my kids who had an affair with the captain, a deckhand who had been married seven times, and another crew guy who ate us out of house and home [laughs].*

Following this two-month journey, Marti spent a year refurbishing her boat and then launched her new company—Pacific Marine Yachts. The early years were rocky: a divorce, a mother with cancer, and loan rejections from 13 banks. While many people might have quit, Marti's dream kept her going. When I sailed with her a few years later, she had four spectacular yachts, 25 full-time employees, 70 part-time employees, and the capacity to entertain 2,500 guests per day. As I disembarked from our voyage, I saw a broken-down wooden boat next to Marti's that seemed out of place. She explained that it was her ex-husband's. Apparently, he thought he could build a better business than she could. Although he may have had more skills and experience, he lacked the most critical ingredients: an incredible zeal for the business and the tenacity to persevere.

After meeting Marti, I quickly realized her remarkable passion and tenacity were not unique to her. All the other successful entrepreneurs I have interviewed have these same two qualities. Mark Young is a friend of mine who earned a master's degree in communication from Michigan State University. His first job was with an advertising agency, where one of his accounts was McDonald's. He quickly decided he would rather own a McDonald's restaurant than do advertising for them. The problem was McDonald's would not consider him for a franchise as long as he was working for one of their vendors. So he quit his job. Next they told him he needed experience working in one of their restaurants before he could apply for a franchise. Even though he took another full-time job to support himself, he worked 20 hours a week for free at a McDonald's that was more than 30 miles from his home. I don't know many people who would work at a fast-food restaurant for free for a year just to be considered for a franchise. Mark has since owned five McDonald's in small towns. His great passion now is to develop team members into excellent leaders and then help them start their own businesses.

Another incredibly passionate and tenacious friend of mine is Jon Schmidt, cofounder of The Piano Guys. Jon gives much of the credit for his success to other people. His dad is a German emigrant who loves music. His sister taught him piano lessons during the early years, and his mom made sure he practiced. Jon's brother Vern also loved music and played a critical role. He would take Jon to music stores and have him play their big grand pianos. He would also bring girlfriends over to the house and ask Jon to play for them. "I'd sit at the piano and think, 'What can I do to impress Vern?'" he says. "His girlfriends would say, 'Stick with this and you'll have the girls after you.' So Vern was a real factor."

When Jon was in the fifth grade, his teacher was an important mentor. She played a piece by Mozart for the class and then challenged Jon to learn it. When he finally played it for his classmates, they went crazy. In sixth grade, his class was waiting for an assembly to start, and the speaker had not shown up yet. His classmates started chanting his name, so he went up and played an amped-up version of "Chopsticks" with seven different themes. Just as before, everyone went crazy.

The following year, he started writing his own songs. He was also performing, accompanying choirs, and still taking lessons. Only now, his mother didn't have to prod him to practice because he had fallen in love with playing music for people. By the time he was 18, he had written 15 songs. Jon still believes these are some of the best pieces he has ever written.

Despite his early success, Jon planned on getting an English degree and an MBA and going into business. He was told it was just too hard to make it in the music world. While working on his bachelor's degree, he was asked to do a benefit concert at his high school. He had just recorded some of his songs and decided to take 40 cassettes to the concert and see what would happen. Around 300 people showed up, he got a standing ovation, and all 40 cassettes sold quickly. A light went on that day, and Jon decided to start doing concerts. Before long he was playing at high schools, colleges, concert halls, and fundraisers. At an event in Colorado he met Lionel Richie and spent two hours with him. He got excellent feedback from Lionel about his music and was now committed to do it full time. He had found his true passion and was going to do whatever it would take to make it work. Although he finished his English degree, he never got an MBA. He was having way too much fun.

On his quest for success, Jon partnered with one of his piano students, Carl Sandquist. Carl was convinced Jon could make it in music and played an invaluable role in his early career. Carl built Jon an attractive website, helped him transcribe his songs to sheet music, and got his music on Pandora. "Without Carl, there is no way I would have survived," Jon says. Partnering with Carl is another example of the way Jon relied on mentors who knew more than he did about certain aspects of his industry. He was willing to learn from everyone he could.

Jon made a decent living for the next 20 years teaching lessons, selling sheet music, doing concerts, and selling CDs. But he was never more than a regional phenomenon in the Intermountain West. He hadn't made it on the national stage. Then he started doing concerts with Steven Sharp Nelson, a superb cellist, a wacky entertainer, and a very funny guy. One day they decided to create a video of themselves playing a song they called "Love Story Meets Viva La Vida." It was Jon's version of "Love Story" by Taylor Swift combined with "Viva La Vida" by Coldplay. They posted the video on YouTube, and Jon emailed the link to the 20,000 fans in his database. Within a month, the video had more than a million views, and they had officially formed The Piano Guys with several other partners. As they say in show business, the rest is history. Jon and his team signed with Sony Entertainment, they do concerts all over the world, and their videos have more than 800 million views on YouTube. While Jon had many chances to quit along the way, his profound zeal for music, and more than two decades of tenacity, finally led to big-time success and international fame.

The Two Critical Qualities

Nearly every thriving entrepreneur I have interviewed has radiated the same two qualities I observed in Marti, Mark, and Jon: zeal for their business and a dogged tenacity to win. Zeal is a joyful and enthusiastic pursuit of some outcome or activity. It is synonymous with passion.

It's a fire that drives the venture. It attracts members to the team, entices customers to buy, helps secure funding, and allows the startup to compete with the giants. Zeal is energy! Zeal is infectious! Zeal is power! It is not possible to start and grow a thriving company without a hearty dose of zeal.

Successful entrepreneurs also possess a teeth-gritting tenacity that won't quit. They find ways to get over mountains, across valleys, and around roadblocks. They simply don't take "no" for an answer. Rather than bail out when the slope gets slippery, they do whatever it takes to make their business work. This often involves working long hours, making personal sacrifices, changing directions, and keeping costs down. This galvanized stance is vital to conquering the rocky road of new venturing.

Early on, I considered zeal and tenacity two separate success factors. I have since discovered that a blend of the two is the essential ingredient. If you have tremendous zeal for your deal but little tenacity, the venture will stagger. The company will also stumble if you have tons of tenacity but come up short on zeal. Hence, zealous tenacity is the critical success factor.

Our Zealously Tenacious Entrepreneurs

Here are some of the stories we collected on our bike ride across America that highlight the importance of zealous tenacity in business building.

Will Lebeda

Will is no stranger to hard work. When he was six years old, his family moved out of their camper and into a single-wide trailer. They didn't have a lot of money, so Will would go out and collect pop cans. The more cans he collected, the better his chance of getting some candy or a toy when his family went shopping. He has worked at some type of job ever since:

> *If I wanted school clothes, I had to help provide extra income. At age 10, I started mowing lawns around the neighborhood. I*

started picking strawberries in the fields at age 11. I learned that the more berries I picked, the more money I could make. At age 12, I was making twice as much as I was the year before. At 13 and 14, I got stronger so I could buck hay. At 15 and 16, I started working places where you needed a work permit. I worked at an Albertsons, then a Wendy's, and then a gas station. By the time I was 18, I was the assistant manager of the station. So I have always held a job regardless of my age because I always needed income. If I worked hard it would pay off. If I didn't work hard, it wouldn't pay off.

Will started working with heavy equipment as he got older. He loved driving big machines, but he hurt his back and found a more suitable job with an insulation company. Before long he was managing the business and took it from four employees to 30. When the recession hit in 2008, the owner started cutting corners to save money and keep his business going. This troubled Will because he took pride in doing excellent work. Several insulation companies went out of business during this time, so he thought there was an opportunity to start his own company, which would allow him to implement his own values of excellence and hard work. He launched Energy Conservation Insulation in Bend, Oregon, in 2009. He felt he could make it with better products, better installations, and better service. His business has not only survived but also thrived. Today, Will has 25 employees and is well-respected by both residential homeowners and commercial builders. Hard work and passion are two important guiding principles in his company. Every morning he tells his team members to not only work hard, but to go out and have fun as well. "If the job is miserable," he says, "you aren't going to keep those employees for very long." In the end, it's what his company contributes to the community that is the most rewarding to Will:

The dollar bill isn't the only thing I work for. I believe by insulating I am not just doing a job; I am making people's lives more comfortable. I also make their living expenses less because we do a better job. I am really passionate about this because it does make a difference. I wake up every day knowing I am going to have a positive effect on someone's life. That is compelling to me.

Nicole Campos

Nicole loves to shop. She spent hours doing it with her mother while growing up. They both love clothing, jewelry, shoes, and accessories. After graduating from college, Nicole moved from Kansas to Las Vegas to work in the promotions industry. On a visit back home to Scott City, her hometown in Kansas, she met an impressive guy, fell in love, and got married. He was teaching in a local school, and Nicole needed something to do. She started selling purses and jewelry out of her basement, and her sales were so strong she launched her new company, Bling, six months later in a small retail space down the street.

Nicole's grandfather was a great mentor. He loaned her $3,000 to buy inventory and cheered her on. She worked hard every day, started going to shows, and developed great relationships with key suppliers. Since most small towns do not have a store like Bling, it became a gathering place. Many customers would come in every week just to chat and see what new merchandise had arrived. Nicole would get their input on desired products and then stock what they wanted to buy. The business model worked really well. Nicole knew that if it worked in Scott City, it would work in other small towns in Kansas. Over the next five years she opened additional stores in Garden City, Manhattan, Hays, and Salina. All this growth was funded with cash flow, and the company is debt-free. Nicole's husband, Mark, has now joined her in the business along with a strong team of store managers. When asked how it all happened, Nicole says:

I had no idea it would take off like this! . . . I didn't have a business plan. All I had was determination. We just worked really hard. We put our heads down, believed in it, and prayed a lot. . . . So you have to put in the time, and you have to make relationships. It doesn't just come.

Nicole wants to continue expanding Bling as a debt-free, family-owned business. "We built this company ourselves, so the passion isn't going anywhere," she says. She also wants to create opportunities to bless the lives of her team members. Most important, she wants her young son to learn that anything is possible with passion and hard work. "If you work really hard, you can have the American Dream. We are proof of that!" she says.

Ryan and Kaylin Chaves

Ryan Chaves was born and raised in Baker City, Oregon. His grandfather owned a grocery store there for many years, and his father still owns a successful consulting firm based there. Although he moved to Los Angeles, Ryan always thought he would go back to Baker City someday to raise his own family. But his wife, Kaylin, had a dream job in Los Angeles. She started working for a modeling agency and then moved to a casting agency. She was placing actors in major roles in Hollywood movies and working with ABC, NBC, CBS, Warner Bros., and Sony. Over time, though, she lost her passion for Los Angeles. She wanted a simpler life and a more attractive place to raise their family. She and Ryan both felt it was time to move to Baker City.

Ryan started working for his father's consulting firm, but their dream was to open their own business in town. They kept asking themselves, "What do people need that they can't get here?" Shoes and clothes kept coming back to them; in particular, shoes, apparel, and equipment in the sporting goods industry. At the time, there was nowhere to buy baseballs, bats, mitts, volleyballs, basketballs, and athletic apparel. Their daughter was playing sports, and they were driving two hours each way to Boise to buy what she needed. As they asked around town, people agreed with them. Baker City needed a sporting goods store.

As Ryan and Kaylin researched the industry, they learned that having top brand names was critical to success. You had to sell brands like Nike, New Balance, Under Armour, and North Face. The problem was that the top brand names have minimum purchase quotas that smaller retailers just can't meet, so they typically don't sell their apparel and equipment to stores in small towns. Ryan and Kaylin were not deterred, though. They decided to open their store, buy brand-name products from third-party wholesalers initially, and then prove they had enough demand to buy these brands directly from the manufacturers. As Ryan reflects, "We didn't realize how hard that was going to be." Nonetheless, they opened Kicks Sportswear on Main Street and had a reasonable first year. People in Baker City were excited they were open.

As their sales grew, Kicks Sportswear acquired the Easton brand and then New Balance. But they really wanted Nike to legitimize their business. Ryan worked on this account tirelessly:

> *We begged and pleaded with them. I can't even begin to tell you how many phone calls and conversations I had with sales reps, regional managers, demographic teams, and analysts. Every year we kept thinking, 'We're going to get Nike.' Two and a half years later, I got a call from them. In my head I kept thinking, 'They are going to tell us we need to discuss it more,' but they said yes! We were all on a Nike high for a week, but that was just the beginning. Nike has multiple divisions, so once you're approved, you can't just start ordering products. We had to set up different accounts with all the different vendors.*

After Ryan and Kaylin acquired Nike, other brands started showing up. They now sell six major brands in their store: Nike, New Balance, North Face, Easton, O'Neill, and Under Armour. This is almost unheard of in a small town with less than 10,000 people. Ryan explains how it happened:

> *It was persistence by us; we sold ourselves. We talked about what having their brand would mean to the community, the outlying communities, and the schools. It just took consistent persistence without upsetting the powers that be. If you make them mad, they are never going to come. So you always have to be nice regardless of what they're saying or how frustrating it gets. But you can't stop moving forward with your business.*

Zealous tenacity is critical to building a strong company. This all-important ingredient for success flows from your underlying purpose, or "why." If your driving purpose is powerful, your zealous tenacity will be fully engaged. If your primary purpose is weak, you may not have enough zealous tenacity to get through the tough times or attract the right team. Here is the formula: purpose + zealous tenacity + other key ingredients = success. This book gives you the "other key ingredients" in the formula.

Although it takes a tremendous amount of effort to build a successful venture, this doesn't mean the work is drudgery. When your purpose is truly inspiring and your zealous tenacity is strong, building an organization is a joyful and engaging endeavor. You work hard because you love what you are doing. You are building your dream, creating jobs, solving an intriguing problem, etc. This is why I hear thriving entrepreneurs say things like, "I've never had so much fun." "I love what I do enough to get up at 4:30 every morning." "This is not work; it's play." I seldom hear winning entrepreneurs say, "This is killing me." "It is far too hard." "I don't know if I can take it any longer." Yet I hear these statements in the corporate world all the time. Many people are just hanging on until something better comes along. In fact, in 2014 the Gallup employee engagement survey showed that approximately 70 percent of U.S. employees were not engaged in their work, and Millennials were the least engaged. Worldwide, 87 percent of employees are not engaged in their work. Entrepreneurs, on the other hand, are the most satisfied with their careers. In my opinion, it is far better to build your own company than it is to drift along aimlessly working for someone else, even if you earn less money doing so.

While building a business can be very engaging and satisfying, let's be realistic. You are going to have some serious setbacks and breakdowns along the way. Your initial market may not be as lucrative as you thought. You may have to redesign products that aren't working. You may hire employees and then struggle to meet payroll. Nothing great is easy to build. Nearly all the successful entrepreneurs I have interviewed have hit bottom a few times. So it is important to be realistic about the work required, it is important to get excited about overcoming the challenges ahead, and it is important to find ways to keep your zealous tenacity alive in the long run. You will need it desperately during the early stages of your business and to get through the doldrums that will inevitably occur during the life of your enterprise.

Maintaining Your Zealous Tenacity

I was so excited to start our 4,000-mile bike ride I could hardly sleep at night. I had trained for a year, found some remarkable entrepreneurs to interview along the way, and enlisted our sponsors. It is hard to describe the flood of emotions I felt when we left the West Coast and started east. That first week across Oregon was our honeymoon. The physical demands were intense, having jumped from 250 miles a week in training to nearly 600 miles, and the 24,763 feet of mountain climbing was no easy feat. But the weather was beautiful, the scenery was spectacular, the people were friendly, the roads were safe, the entrepreneurs were plentiful, and the wildlife was abundant. We even saw a baby deer just minutes after it was born in the forest. That week could not have been more exhilarating.

Idaho was also stunning, with great weather and welcoming people. Although the motorhome broke down on White Bird Hill, it's a thing, not a person, so it really wasn't that bad. And Mary and I had an unforgettable experience riding through the mountains on our own. One of my best memories was watching Mary catch a three-foot salmon in the river behind our hotel in the tiny town of Riggins. At the time, it seemed like one of the best meals I had ever eaten.

Our honeymoon ended abruptly in Montana and Wyoming. While the previous week had been unseasonably warm, this was one of the coldest June weeks in years. The unpredictability of the vast American wilderness came home to roost. One day I stopped at a convenience store in Twin Bridges, Montana, after riding for 30 miles in freezing rain. When the clerk asked me what in the world I was doing riding in this rain, I couldn't answer her because my face was so cold. I think she thought I was an escapee from a mental institution. The next 30 miles were worse: Hail pelted my face and snow covered the road. The last part of the day was a long climb over a mountain with 6 to 12 percent grades. I had to fight to keep my bike in the tire tracks the cars were making in the snow. It was absolutely miserable. I kept thinking,

"I wanted to ride my bike across America. I didn't want to climb Mt. Everest."

The foul weather continued into Wyoming. We had to cancel rides, miss interviews, and alter our schedule. When we got to Jackson Hole, all the RV parks were full, so we stayed in a rundown camp 20 miles outside town, which was unbelievably expensive. We were paying for the Ritz-Carlton but staying in a Motel 6. The darkness was so thick you could touch it. The zealous tenacity we had enjoyed across Oregon and Idaho had clearly packed up and gone home. We were all seriously questioning our "why." We were also only four hours from our home in Salt Lake City, which was weighing on our minds.

After a long period of silence, I suggested we have what my sons call a "feeling circle." They hate these because you have to express your feelings about a certain person or experience. Trying to bring our severely deflated team back from the precipice, I suggested we each describe a high and a low point during the past week. Shawn's high was interviewing the owners of the Buffalo Meat Company; his low was participating in the feeling circle. Mary's high was swimming in a great pool in Jackson Hole; her low was seeing how stressed out Jay was becoming. Jay said he felt no highs or lows, just an overwhelming buzz of numbness. He had been riding in horrible weather, almost lost his fingers to frostbite, and was shooting video all day and editing well into the night.

Just expressing our negative emotions helped a lot. More important, we created a new plan for going forward. We discussed our purpose, and concluded we all still believed in it strongly. We altered our expectations about the challenges ahead and revised our schedule to allow more time for breaks and fun. We agreed Jay should focus on behind-the-scenes videos and not feel pressured to create full documentaries about every entrepreneur we interviewed. Finally, we decided we would not ride our bikes on days where our chances of dying were high. The plan worked! The next day was a fantastic 124-mile ride from Moran Junction to Lander, Wyoming. We climbed a scenic pass at 9,500 feet and then rode into Lander to interview some amazing entrepreneurs. We were back in the game.

Our breakdown in Montana and Wyoming was not unlike what entrepreneurs experience from time to time while building their dream. Chris Michel, founder of Military.com, told us he was ready to give his business away for one dollar several months before selling it to Monster Worldwide, Inc. for $40 million. Tony Conza, founder of Blimpie, told me he completely lost his passion for the business after he had a couple hundred stores. So he went to Tanzania for three weeks and had a long meeting with himself. He redefined his purpose, found a new passion, set some serious goals, came home, and opened 1,000 stores over the next few years. According to Tony, "You don't survive under the conditions we were in without having real passion to be successful. It was definitely the passion and excitement that kept us going." Having heard hundreds of stories like this, I have observed five things successful entrepreneurs do to keep zealous tenacity alive.

1. Revisit Your Purpose

As mentioned in the previous chapter, it is important to constantly revisit your "why" as part of the planning process. Make sure it is still engaging. Decide if it needs to be altered or amended. Reflect on other compelling reasons for building your business. If you fail to do this at regular intervals, you can get hung up in the "what" and "how" of running your company and forget why you started it in the first place. Remember, if you have a strong "why," you can get through any "what" and "how." This process will keep your zealous tenacity engaged.

While revisiting your purpose, also reflect on the advantages of business ownership. Remember that boss who drove you crazy on your last job? Well, now you get to call the shots. You can create your own strategy. You can hire who you want. You can make changes quickly. You can fix things that don't work. You can operate according to your own values. You can build equity in your business. And you can go to your kids' soccer games and school assemblies. Reflecting on the advantages of ownership—as opposed to being unengaged in a corporate structure—will help keep your zealous tenacity alive.

2. Manage Your Thoughts

During our bike ride we found it far more helpful to ask each other, "How are you thinking today?" rather than "How are you feeling?" If we got out of bed and focused on our sore legs, the size of the mountains we had to climb, or how demanding it would be to ride 100 miles again today after doing it yesterday, the day would be far more difficult. On the other hand, if we got up each day and had encouraging thoughts, like "I'm sore but I can do this," or "We'll just take it 10 miles at a time," or "We'll take breaks if we need to," we had much better days. Positive thinking became our greatest ally.

A great deal of research supports the concept that we feel the way we think. When we have negative or scary thoughts, various chemicals like cortisol and adrenaline are released in the brain, causing feelings of anxiety and depression. When we think positive and optimistic thoughts, happy neurotransmitters are released, helping us feel better. As Viktor Frankl concludes in *Man's Search for Meaning*, we cannot always control our external circumstances, but we can control our mental responses to those circumstances. The ability to choose our thoughts is one of the greatest freedoms of our mortal existence. The successful entrepreneurs we interviewed are masters of optimistic thinking, which keeps their zealous tenacity burning. The key is to focus on all the ways you can make something work rather than the reasons it won't work.

In addition, managing your expectations plays a critical role in staying passionately engaged. At the beginning of our trip, I thought we would have mostly great weather with a few bad days. After our bout with nature in Montana and Wyoming, we realized that any day could be tough. When we started preparing for battle each day and got excited to overcome all the trials we might face, we had much better days. It's funny how the weather got worse, but our ability to handle it joyfully improved significantly. I have seen this same phenomenon in the lives of aspiring entrepreneurs. Those who think it should be easy often give up prematurely. Those who know it can be hard and get excited to overcome the challenges do much better in the long run.

3. Set and Achieve Goals

In Chapter 6, we talked about creating a two- or three-year vision for your company and then setting four to six goals each year to help you achieve that vision. Nothing is more motivating than consistent progress toward a desirable destination. Entrepreneurs who set and achieve goals that are linked to an exciting vision have far more energy than those who don't. In business, you are either going forward or backwards, and it is much more invigorating to go forward.

Here is the simple goal-setting process I have seen used by hundreds of successful entrepreneurs. First, they set attainable goals that are consistent with their longer-term vision. Second, they devise a method for accomplishing these goals. Third, they work their plan with great passion and tenacity. Soon they achieve their goals and enjoy the rewards of success, which increases their confidence and motivation to begin the process again. I call these cycles "propelling events," because they continue to propel winning entrepreneurs to higher levels following each round of success. This process does wonders for keeping zealous tenacity burning in growing companies. It is illustrated in Figure 7–1 on page 118.

4. Take Regular Breaks

Launching a new business is like getting on the freeway and putting the pedal to the metal. If you don't stop occasionally, you run out of gas or burn out the engine. Some entrepreneurs I know gave up everything for their business for years. Looking back, they feel they could have been just as successful, much less stressed, and a great deal happier if they had taken some time off from their enterprise every now and then.

We are all better at the things we love if we take regular breaks from them. We are better athletes when we take rest days from exercise. We are better students when we take study breaks. We are better parents when we also make time for ourselves. And we are better entrepreneurs when we take time off from our ventures. Taking a break gives us a rest, rejuvenates us, and prepares us to go back to what we love doing. Even if you don't think you need breaks, take them anyway.

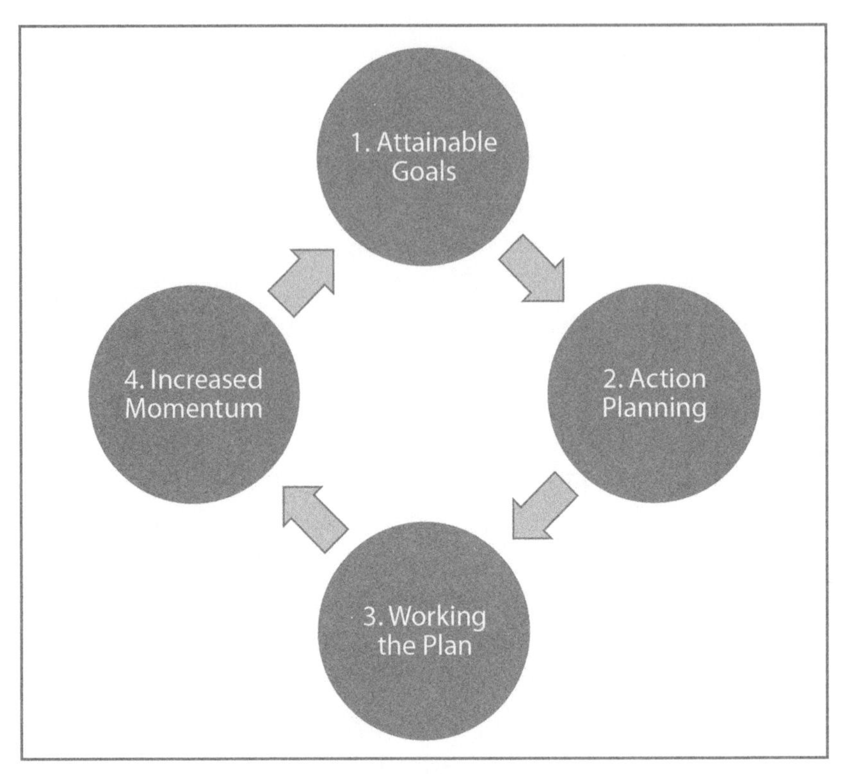

Figure 7–1: **The Entrepreneurial Goal-Setting Process**

The successful entrepreneurs we met across America are excellent role models for merging livelihood and lifestyle. They continue to do the things they love, whether it is skiing, boating, hiking, traveling, or time with family. While their entrepreneurial engines are cooling down, they are rejuvenating their passion for driving.

5. Always Stay Humble

Before starting our cross-country adventure, I expected to suffer a great deal. As it turned out, the bike ride wasn't as hard as we thought it would be. The first few weeks were very demanding, but our daily rides got easier and easier as our bodies adjusted. By the time we got to the beach in Virginia, we felt we could turn around and ride back home, no problem.

The only time I experienced extreme suffering on our trip was my own fault. I brought it upon myself for three days in the Ozark Mountains in Missouri. While the mountains in the west are long, gradual grades, the Ozarks are a never-ending series of spikes that go up and down all day long. The elevation map of the area looks like a series of jagged shark's teeth, and they bite hard. You climb up a super steep hill with a 10 to 20 percent grade, and then fly down the other side at 45 miles an hour—and you do it again and again and again. One morning we climbed 10 of these in 10 miles; we must have climbed several hundred in three days.

By the time we got to Missouri, I was feeling like a superhero. We had ridden 2,500 miles, and I was flying like a man half my age. I crossed the entire state of Kansas in my big chain ring up front, which is the hardest set of gears, and I committed to do the same thing across Missouri. I guess I thought it would be some kind of status symbol. Here is the problem: Muscles under severe strain produce lactic acid, which results in fatigue and post-workout soreness. So when you use your harder gears on steep hills, you burn out your legs. The much smarter strategy is to spin up big hills at a higher cadence in your easier gears, which relies on your cardiovascular strength and preserves your legs to ride another day. I knew this from past experience, but I thought I was now in an elite class. So the first day in the Ozarks, I hammered my big gears all day long until I realized how silly I was being. When I finally switched to my easier spinning gears, the damage had already been done. My legs were fried for the next two days, with many more spikes to climb. So I got cocky in Kansas, and hubris trashed my legs in the Ozarks.

REFLECTION

Assessing Your Zealous Tenacity

Here is the important lesson: Building a business is like running a marathon, not a sprint. You have to run at a steady pace over time or you will burn yourself out. If you feel you have finally "arrived," you are vulnerable to fall. I have seen hubris trash a lot of businesses over the years. In contrast, the thriving entrepreneurs we met across America are pretty humble about their successes. They know there are always more spikes in the road ahead, and they are excited to deal with these challenges. This modest attitude keeps zealous tenacity alive. Pride, on the other hand, may cause it to dissipate when you need it most. Remember, your business is a continual work in progress, so enjoy the ride. Believing there is no finish line will keep you fully engaged in the long run. The questions below will help you assess the strength of your zealous tenacity. Ask yourself these questions from time to time to keep your fire burning.

1. Can you clearly articulate the purpose for building your business?
2. What negative thoughts do you repeat that may be holding you back?
3. What critical goals are you pursuing that will keep your zealous tenacity strong?
4. What outside hobbies and activities will you maintain while building your business?
5. What are you doing to stay humble about the successes you are having?

CHAPTER

8

Build a Community of Raving Fans

"The link between our consumer and ENVE is of paramount importance. In fact, we don't even call them a consumer; we just say, 'Welcome to the ENVE family.' They are an extension of who we are, and we do everything we can to understand and meet their needs. . . . It's a really intimate relationship."

—Sarah Lehman, CEO of ENVE Composites

Every state we visited was unique, but Kentucky was the most like a foreign country—at least the part of the state we traveled through. At first we thought they were speaking a foreign language, but once we adjusted to their pronunciation of vowels, we understood them just fine. While the hills of Kentucky are absolutely stunning, what stood out the most was the incredible warmth and kindness of the people. Everywhere we went, they were genuinely interested in our adventure and wanted to make sure we felt welcome in their community. Here are a few examples.

Mary, Jay, and I were riding from Berea to Hazard, a 100-mile ride with more than 8,000 feet of climbing. It was the most elevation gain in a single day on our entire trip. Shawn drove the bus into Hazard to pick up a package from one of our sponsors at the post office. He punched the address into his phone and drove into town. He took a right-hand turn up a steep road that became narrower and narrower; then he took a sharp left up an even steeper hill with houses, cars, and dumpsters along the road. The motorhome barely fit by inches on either side. At the top of this hill was a sharp hairpin turn the bus would never make. Shawn quickly realized he was stuck on the mountain: he couldn't go forward, he couldn't turn around, and he couldn't back down without crashing into everything he had just passed on the way up. He cursed the powers that be and put his head down on the steering wheel, completely incapable of movement. He momentarily considered leaving the bus on the mountain and finding a family in a hollow that would hide him for a few months.

Before long, a large crowd was gathering to find out why a guy from Utah had driven a 33-foot motorhome onto their mountainside. A gentleman knocked on the window.

"Hi, I'm Mark," he said. "I think you made a wrong turn."

You got that right, thought Shawn.

"You can't go forward, and you can't turn. You need to back out. Let me help."

Mark got behind the motorhome on his scooter and slowly guided Shawn backwards down the hill. A couple of times he had to stop cars and send them back down the mountain. While this was going on, hordes of people were cheering Shawn on.

"You can do this, brother!"

"You are doing awesome, man!"

"You got this, buddy."

Relying on his mirrors, the backup camera, Mark's commands, and the crowd, Shawn was able to thread the needle down the two narrow hills. When they finally got to the bottom, Mark led Shawn to the post office on a much flatter road. He even went inside and waited in line with Shawn to make sure everything turned out OK. According to Shawn, "It was an awesome show of support from people I had never met. They were all too willing to help a stranger in need. I couldn't have gotten out of that situation without Mark's help." When Shawn thanked Mark for spending his afternoon helping him, Mark replied, "It was the right thing to do."

On another occasion, we pulled into Elkhorn City late in the day. We needed something to eat, so we stopped at the Subway sandwich shop in town. Shawn started talking to a guy who introduced himself as Mayor Taylor, the mayor of the city. He was excited we had stopped in his town and asked where we were staying that night. At that point we had no plans. He told us we could park our motorhome at city hall just down the street or at Breaks Interstate Park a few miles down the highway. We thanked him and told him we would check out city hall. When we got there, the assistant fire chief and several of his men were out front waiting for us. The mayor had called him and told him to take care of us. After a delightful conversation about the area, we decided to go to the park, since there were no power or water hookups at city hall. They agreed it was a better solution and gave us directions.

Breaks Interstate Park is the Grand Canyon of Kentucky and Virginia. It sits right on the border above a spectacular gorge. It has cottages around a lake and RV hookups on the hillside. When we got there, the park manager was waiting for us. The assistant fire chief had called the park ranger, and the ranger went to the RV park to make sure there was a space for us. He then told the park manager we were coming and to treat us well. The manager gave us a beautiful site on top of the mountain overlooking the gorge.

That's how things went all across Kentucky. People wanted to visit with us, went out of their way to help, and made sure we had a great time in their town. There may be plenty of feuds in some of the hollows in the hills (pronounced "hollers"), but we felt nothing but kindness and generosity from everyone we met. Although I am excited to return to every state we visited, I am particularly interested in spending more time in Kentucky, with its extraordinary terrain and incredibly gracious people. We are now raving fans of the state.

Creating a Tribal Mentality

In their book *Tribal Leadership*, Dave Logan, John King, and Halee Fischer-Wright argue that organizations are made up of tribes of people. Organizations with healthy and cohesive tribes are more successful than organizations with dysfunctional tribes. The book outlines five stages of tribal functioning, from very low to very high. At stage one, tribal members hate themselves and the organization; their mantra is "Life sucks." At stage two, members are disengaged, apathetic, and resistant to management initiatives; their mantra is "My life sucks." At stage three, people pursue self-interest in the hierarchy, but don't work together as a team; their mantra is "I'm great." At stage four, members enjoy working together for the benefit of the overall organization; their mantra is "We're great." At stage five, tribal members are fully engaged, make innovative contributions, and strive to have a broader impact in the world; their mantra is "Life's great." The authors conclude that 76 percent of all organizations have cultures in the first three stages; 22 percent have cultures in stage four; and only 2 percent have cultures in stage five. Obviously, organizations at stages four and five are far more successful than organizations with cultures at the lower stages.

The entrepreneurs we visited across the country are striving to create a stage five culture—and they are succeeding. Their business purpose is clear, team members buy into their vision, and they are trying to impact the broader community. Even more important than team culture is the tribal building these entrepreneurs are doing with the people they serve. They have extended the tribal leadership concept to their community of customers. In order to build a strong tribe of raving fans, your internal culture must first be functioning at a highly cohesive level. In Chapter 5, we outlined important principles for developing a strong supporting cast of team members. This is a prerequisite for having loyal fans who love your business.

This chapter extends the tribal leadership concept to building your customer base. It will help you build a community of raving fans who will always choose your company when they need the products or services you sell. Let's start with the simple model in Figure 8–1 on page 125 that illustrates the various levels of community building companies do with their customers.

Level 1: Tolerate Your Customers

I actually once had the manager of a business tell me, "This would be a great place to work if it weren't for the customers." In other words,

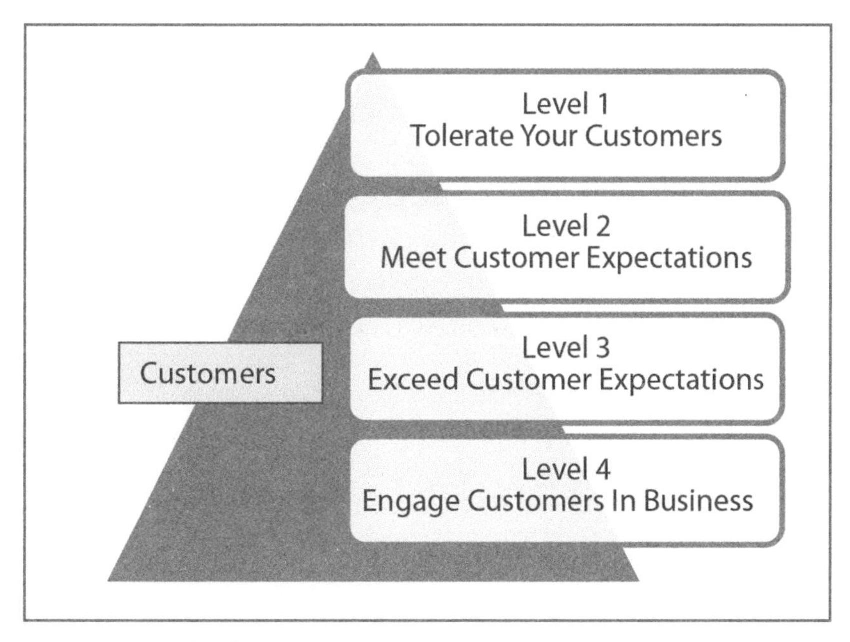

Figure 8–1: **Levels of Customer Service**

customers were pests that got in her way when she had more important things to do. It was a pain for her to take care of them. I am sure people who patronized that business felt the lack of passion for their presence. Notice in the model above that these types of organizations only gain the very small tip of the customer pyramid. No one goes to these companies unless there is nowhere else to get the product or service. In our highly competitive business landscape, however, there are few companies with no competitors. Consequently, this level of service usually only exists in government agencies. I am thinking about my last visit to the Department of Motor Vehicles.

Level 2: Meet Customer Expectations

Customer expectations form an important baseline in the business world. Nearly all customers approach companies with preconceived notions of how they should be treated. If their expectations are not met, they are dissatisfied. They complain, tell all their friends, and never return to that business. If their expectations are met, things are OK. They are not jumping for joy, but they are basically satisfied. Level 2 companies go to great lengths to make sure all their customers are satisfied with the service they receive. Since a major objective is to mitigate the negative impact of unhappy customers, they often create a host of rules and policies for handling various transactions to make sure everyone will be satisfied. The problem is, satisfied customers are not always loyal customers. They patronize competitors' businesses as well. In other words, being satisfied is the same as being neutral. Consequently, Level 2 companies have to constantly play the marketing manipulation game to entice customers to buy their products and services.

Level 3: Exceed Customer Expectations

I recently visited an entrepreneur who owns a small lumberyard in Manila in the Philippines. She is doing very well even though she has several nearby competitors. When I asked her about her success, she said, "Everyone likes me more than them." I asked her why, and she said, "I get what customers want, I cut their wood for free, and I deliver it for free. No one else will do this for them." This is what it takes to produce raving customers and long-term loyalty: providing more than people expect to receive. I call this "mind-boggling service" because it violates customers' preprogrammed expectations on the high side. When customers receive service beyond their imagination, they rave about it to all their friends, come back again and again, become advocates for the company, and even feel guilty if they visit a competitor's business. The successful entrepreneurs we interviewed understand this concept well. They offer excellent prices, lots of personal interaction, extra services for free, astounding speed of delivery, superb customer support, money-back guarantees, etc. Overshooting customer expectations is a critical step in building a tribe of raving fans. It gives you a large piece of the customer pyramid.

Level 4: Engage Customers in Business

The ultimate way to build a tribe of loyal followers is to include customers in the actual development of your business whenever possible. When you collaborate with them in a way that meets both their needs and yours, it binds you together in a meaningful long-term relationship. In a small way, they come to feel that your company is also their company. You have seen how Nicole Campos of Bling interacts with customers regularly to determine what products they want her to order. Melanie Marlow and Mike Domeyer of Shasta Leatherworks have detailed conversations with their customers about dimensions, function, and color before building them exactly what they want. And Steve Sullivan of Stio has organized a group of Ambassadors who test his products, provide input on his business, and promote his brand. I did something similar in our frozen dessert company: I created a group of "customers as partners" who came to regular taste panels, helped create our product line, and gave input on other aspects of our business. In return, I offered them VIP cards that entitled them to half-price on all our products for a year. These fans became our greatest advocates with our broader customer base. Coming to one of our stores with their friends, family members, or colleagues and pulling out their VIP card was a heady experience for them.

When you exceed customer expectations (Level 3) and include them in your business in some way (Level 4), you build a strong community of raving fans, particularly if they are excited about the driving purpose behind your business. As you can see in the model in Figure 8-1, these two levels of service give you the biggest share of the customer pyramid. The experiences I have had with companies that provide this type of service have bound me to them for life. Here is an experience I had with Southwest Airlines.

During a fun weekend in San Francisco, my young son Tyler bought a wooden sword in Chinatown. When we got to the airport, we were told he couldn't carry it on the plane. Since it was too long to fit in his suitcase, we had to put it in a box for the cargo hold. We also had to sign a waiver releasing the airline from any damage that might occur. Of course, when we arrived in Salt Lake City, the sword was broken into three pieces. After we got home, Tyler disappeared into my office to write a letter to Colleen Barrett, the CEO of Southwest Airlines. It said in part:

I ask you please out of the goodness of your heart to send a sad boy the $20 refund he deserves. Not that it counts for much, but I will never fly on your airline again, and I will encourage everyone I know not to fly with you.

A few weeks later we got a letter and a large box from Colleen Barrett's assistant, replying:

I humbly acknowledge that we failed miserably in meeting your expectations last month. I am so sorry you are left with such a dismal view of our customer service. I promise you this experience is not typical of our company or our people. I'm hopeful you will give us another chance to create some positive memories with us. With this in mind, I've enclosed a replacement sword that I hope is received in the spirit intended. Your confidence in our service is precious to us, and we want nothing more than to restore your faith in Southwest Airlines.

The accompanying gift was a replica of Excalibur worth around $100. Needless to say, Tyler was absolutely thrilled and exchanged a picture and several more letters with Colleen's assistant. How many multibillion-dollar companies would do this for a small boy? It's obvious why Southwest is one of the most successful airlines in the history of aviation. Their driving purpose—"dedication to the highest quality of Customer Service delivered with a sense of warmth, friendliness, individual pride, and Company Spirit"—has sustained them for decades.

Our Tribe-Building Entrepreneurs

All the entrepreneurs we met across the country provide Level 3 service; they constantly exceed their customers' expectations, giving them more than they expect to receive. Many of them are also striving for Level 4 customer service, including their customers in the very fabric and development of their business. Here are some brief quotes from entrepreneurs you have met in previous chapters:

Dave Twombly, founder of Central Coast Disposal: *I believe in what I am doing. It's not just a business I'm running. I believe I am helping the community. If the competition was the only business in town, people would not get the kind of service they are getting now. Big companies say, 'If you don't have your garbage at the curb or if a car is in the way, we don't pick it up.' We don't do that here. If you forget your garbage and it's sitting by your garage, our guys will get out of the truck, walk up to your house, get your garbage, and dump it. We do that because we love the community. These are our neighbors.*

Omer Orian, founder of Off the Waffle: *Every customer walks out happy no matter what. You don't let them leave unless they have a smile on their face, and they are going to come back. We empower our crew members to make sure our customers are happy. If you need to give them a free beer, you are empowered to do that. If the food was 20 minutes late, you can give them a gift card so they will come back. If you are unsure it was the right thing, let us know and we'll give you feedback. But when in doubt, just do it, make sure they are happy. That's the bottom line.*

Amy Gardner, founder of Scarpa: *I'm not here to sell them a pair of shoes. I'm here to sell something for 20 years, so I'm not going to sell something that doesn't fit, that doesn't look good, that's poor quality, or that's not right for what they need. If something falls apart, I'm on the phone with the vendor trying to get it fixed. If the vendor won't deal with it, I take responsibility for it even though it's not my fault. . . . Letting customers know they are valuable is far more important than the few dollars I'll recognize. And it goes beyond daily interaction. It's letting working women know, 'I understand you're busy, don't be shy. Call me. I will deliver to your office whatever you need so you can try it on.' Whatever it takes! I'm just respectful of where they are in their lives, and I'm going to do what I can to make it easier for them to be my customer.*

It's not surprising that a group of Amy's customers bought gift certificates for $5,000 and $10,000 in advance to help her raise funds during the recession. They all love the service she provides and want her to stay in business. Here are some more entrepreneurs we met across the country who do a remarkable job building a community of raving fans.

Bill Bezuk

Bill Bezuk knows a lot of people who want to move to the country and enjoy the good life. Unfortunately, this is not always possible due to work, school, family, and other obligations. Bill's mission is to help you enjoy the best of both worlds: rural living in an urban location. His business, The Eugene Backyard Farmer, helps you create a small farm in your own backyard. This is called "urban farming": taking the practices of rural farming and shrinking them down to a much smaller scale. Bill doesn't just teach you how to do this; he sells everything you need to get started: baby chicks, ducklings, turkeys, coops, beehives, tools, fertilizers, a variety of feeds, and all kinds of veggie seeds.

Bill started his Eugene, Oregon, business in 2010 to serve the growing number of people who want to plant their own garden and eat their own food. His business has grown steadily over the past five years, both in revenue and in new products. One of his more recent additions is a chicken hotel. When people who have chickens go out of town, they need someone to care for them. If they can't find a caretaker, they bring them to Bill's chicken hotel. Unfortunately, the week we visited Bill someone had jumped his fence, broken the lock on one of the coops, and stolen one of the chickens. Bill has a vast community of faithful customers, and he stays connected with them through social media. So when he put the word out that one of his chickens had been stolen, people wanted to help. Within a few days his posting had been shared more than a thousand times and garnered hundreds of comments. Within the week, Bill had some good news to report to his faithful community:

> *Great news! Our stolen chicken post was viewed by so many people, and the hen was spotted several times wandering downtown. It made its way to 11th and Olive, where the good folks at Healthy Paws Wellness Center caught her and kept her safe until we arrived. She*

is back with her flock, and we are certain she has some stories to tell. . . . The donations we have received are so appreciated. Thanks again for proving that Eugene is a truly amazing community.

David Tibbitts

Dave Tibbitts is another entrepreneur who has built a tribe of raving fans. He made some money in California real estate, but his life was pretty stressful. He wanted a different lifestyle, so he moved to Jackson Hole, Wyoming. When he arrived, he heard that a whitewater rafting business was for sale. It included two permits to run the Snake River, which are very hard to obtain. Dave bought the business for $65,000. It was located at Alpine Junction, about 35 miles south of Jackson Hole. He wanted to move the business into town, which meant he needed some land and a building. A gentleman in his 80s agreed to lease Dave a piece of property on the main highway for $500 per month. A friend was tearing down some old buildings at an Executive Inn and gave him one for free. Dave now had his land and building and hung out his sign: Jackson Hole Whitewater.

Dave has operated his business for more than 30 years and has built a remarkable reputation and fan base through superb customer service. Dave's goal is to have every customer say, "Our whitewater trip was the highlight of our vacation!" Here is how Dave accomplished this right from the beginning. First, when people called for information about a river trip, he would spend a great deal of time on the phone with them helping them plan the rest of their vacation in Jackson. He would make recommendations for hotels, restaurants, hikes, and shows and provide phone numbers. When they finally arrived for their river trip, they would tell Dave, "You've made our vacation so great, you should really be a travel agent."

Dave would also accommodate customers every way he could to make sure they had a fabulous experience. If they called at 11:30 at night, he would get up and book them a trip. If they showed up on the wrong day, he would find a way to take them down the river. After each trip, he would also spend a lot of time with his guests to make sure they were having fun. One time he was cooking steaks for his afternoon group, and a doctor on the trip asked him if he was the owner. Dave said, "Yeah, how'd you know? I am just cooking." The doctor replied:

> *No, you're telling jokes, flipping garlic bread to people, and having such a good time. You know something? I make about $600,000 a year, and I would trade my practice, my income, my home, everything for your lifestyle. Do you know how fortunate you are to have a business you run in Jackson Hole in the summertime where you float the river, wear Tevas and shorts, get real tan, and then ski a couple of months?*

Dave replied, "I realize that, so I won't be trading you." Dave's son, Jeff, now runs the business and follows the same practices his father started. So plan a trip to Jackson and spend a day with Jackson Hole Whitewater. It will be the highlight of your trip.

Tim Reiman

Tim Reiman and Brad Henderson loved playing whiffle ball in high school. A man in the neighborhood owned a large abandoned field, and the boys asked him if they could play there. He told them they could do whatever they wanted with the field, and they turned it into one of the finest whiffle ball fields in the nation. Tim and Brad cut down three feet of grass, put up a fence, added benches, and put in lights and a 20-foot flagpole. They even persuaded a sod farm to sell them 600 square yards of the same Bermuda Quickstand sod that the St. Louis Cardinals play on for half-price. To fund their dream they raised money and sold advertising to local businesses on the outfield fence. When the field was finished, they ran tournaments every year with corporate and college teams. Tim and Brad continued to operate the field through their high school and college years.

While attending Southern Illinois University in Carbondale, Tim studied prelaw and Brad studied marketing. One night over drinks and a bucket of chicken wings, they talked about starting their own business. They both loved sports and pizza, so they decided to open a pizza shop. For years they had been referred to as the "whiffle boys," so they decided to capitalize on their personal brand. They opened their first Whiffle Boy's Pizza shop in Murphysboro. Tim managed the operation and Brad did the marketing. After a year, Brad followed a girl to Texas and left the business.

Three years later, Tim decided to open a second location in Carbondale, a much bigger town. He learned a valuable lesson. Carbondale was flooded with national pizza chains, and it was hard to gain traction. Since the students were coming and going each year, they tended to support the brands they knew. In contrast, Murphysboro has less than 10,000 residents and is an entirely different market. Tim closed the Carbondale store after one year:

> *In this town, people go out of their way to go to the local places more than they do the big-time pizza places. The amount of support we get is great. People really get excited when we do stuff here. I am thinking about knocking this building down and building a new one. I talked to the mayor, and he said, 'We'll do whatever we have to, we're going to support you. Whatever you need, just call my cell phone, and we'll take care of it.' The people in Murphysboro have just been amazing.*

Tim has decided to stick to smaller towns because it is easier to build a community of raving fans. He and an employee opened a second location in Anna, Illinois, a city of 4,300 people. Both locations are doing great. In addition to staying in small towns where they are needed and appreciated, Tim works hard to build a loyal tribe of followers. When schools and churches need to feed a lot of kids, he gives them significant discounts on pizza. He also sponsors teams and supports most fundraisers in town. Most important, Tim gets to know his customers personally. His sophisticated point-of-sale system tracks customers' pizza preferences, buying patterns, and favorite sports teams. If someone loves a certain type of pizza, he can create ten coupons for it and send them to that customer. He can also print the logos of his customers' favorite teams on their coupons and gift certificates. He is constantly looking for ways to build personal relationships to make him the main pizza provider in town, and his plan is working. He is doing big business in a small town with loyal fans who love him.

ENVE Composites

Cousins Brett and Taylor Satterthwaite started a business called Edge Products in 1999 that designed and sold after-market electronic devices to improve engine performance and fuel efficiency. Brett and Taylor have always loved recreational cycling, so after they sold the company in 2005 they opened a bike shop together—Biker's Edge in Kaysville, Utah. At this same time, the cousins started a carbon-fiber business, ENVE Composites, that did contract engineering for other companies. They created an icepick handle for Black Diamond and a carbon ski binding for Burton Snowboards; they also started designing and building state-of-the-art carbon-fiber wheels for bicycles.

Paul and Sarah Lehman had been partners in Edge Products—Paul was an investor, and Sarah managed the marketing—and the two of them joined Brett and Taylor at ENVE. With an MBA from Harvard, Sarah has been the CEO since 2010. She was named CEO of the year by *Utah Business* magazine in 2014. ENVE now makes some of the finest bicycle wheels in the world. As mentioned in Chapter 3, we met the stuntman who played Bigfoot in *Harry and the Hendersons* in Idaho; he was riding on a set of ENVE wheels. When I asked him how he liked them, he raved about the wheels and the company for ten minutes. I have gotten this same response from everyone else I have met that uses ENVE wheels. The company has done a number of things to create such a strong following of raving fans.

As the company was starting to gain traction, the team had to decide whether to manufacture in the U.S. or Asia. They agonized over this for months. Since all their competitors are manufacturing in Asia, they felt they had to do the same to stay competitive on price. But they just didn't feel good about it and decided to stay in the U.S.—no matter what. The strategy was all about innovation, quality, and customer satisfaction. When you manufacture in Asia, you create a single design for the year, place a large batch order, get it four months later, and are stuck with what you get, even if the quality is poor or changes are needed. With their own domestic facility, they can design quickly, test immediately, manufacture smaller batches, solve problems fast, and redesign in record time.

The second thing the ENVE team did was create a powerful culture for mind-boggling customer service. Everyone in the company knows that customers are members of the ENVE family. They are an extension of everything the company is trying to achieve. Team members and customers communicate often and collaborate on product development and improvements—Level 4 in our customer service model. It is a very intimate relationship.

The third thing the team has done is create a host of systems that clearly communicate that the customer comes first. They have extended their initial two-year warranty to a five-year warranty with no questions asked. They have added a lifetime crash replacement program. And they avoid policies that prevent employees from quickly solving customer problems. Sarah explains:

> *The line of defense always starts and ends with the person handling the issue. . . . The first person who sees the snake has the authority to kill the snake. The thing I can't stand with other companies is to be told, 'No, that's not our policy, I can't help you.' Those words aren't allowed here.*

ENVE's innovative design and manufacturing process, its strong culture of complete customer delight, and its systems that promote spectacular customer service have made ENVE a world-class producer of state-of-the-art bicycle wheels. We used them on our ride across America and fell in love with them the first day. ENVE is by far my favorite brand of wheels. I won't ever use another brand.

The Service Is in the System

It's easy to provide amazing customer service when you are the only one responsible for it. Some of the business owners we interviewed are "solopreneurs" and have built remarkable long-term relationships with their customers. However, others are growing and have 40, 50, or 60 employees. It is harder to maintain that level of service when you are no longer the solo service provider. Successful entrepreneurs not only provide mind-boggling service early on, but they also create brilliant systems for maintaining dazzling service as their business grows, so every customer will have the same experience regardless of who serves them. You have seen how the entrepreneurs above and others in this book accomplish this:

- They hire decent people who also believe in their mission.
- They create a strong culture that focuses on customers as partners.
- They lead by example and serve customers themselves.
- They shun policies that might interfere with great service.
- They give team members the autonomy to solve customers' problems.
- They have constant dialogue about cases that arise with customers.

Mind-boggling customer service was the top priority for our frozen dessert company, but as we hired hundreds of teenage employees, we realized our emphasis on exceptional service was slipping. Here's what we did. First, we asked our customers to help us define "mind-boggling" service from their perspective. We wanted to know what it would take to significantly exceed their expectations. Next, we created a "Profile of Mind-Boggling Customer Service" that outlined the answers they gave us and committed to do these things with every customer who patronized our business. Finally, we used this profile to drive every human resource process in our company. Here's how it worked:

1. We *hired* team members who could naturally perform the behaviors in the profile.
2. We *trained* all team members to implement the profile with customers.
3. We *evaluated* team members regularly on how well they were executing the profile.
4. We *rewarded* team members based on how well they scored on the profile evaluation.

Our customer service system is depicted in Figure 8–2. Notice how the Profile of Mind-Boggling Customer Service connects all the human resource processes we implemented in the organization.

So how did our system work? It was an ongoing challenge because it was implemented through hundreds of teenagers. Nonetheless, we believe our customer service was far superior to our competitors in the

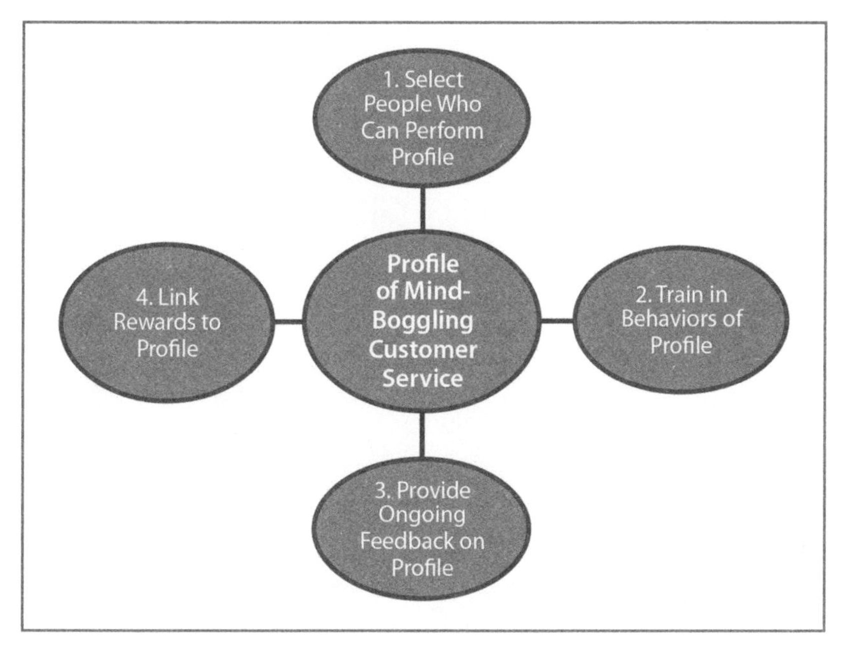

Figure 8–2: **Model of Mind-Boggling Customer Service**

food industry. We witnessed remarkable efforts to exceed customer expectations on a daily basis. This is the important lesson: Systems will deliver whatever behavior they are designed to produce. If you only pay lip service to great customer service, it isn't going to happen, but if you create systems to promote great customer service, it will happen. The service is in the system.

Building Your Community

Competition is intense in every industry. More businesses are providing more products through more channels than ever before, and customers ultimately buy from the companies they like the most. Hence, customer service is the battleground of our era. Successful entrepreneurs first discover ways to give customers much more than they expect to receive and then create systems for perpetuating exceptional service on an ongoing basis as the company grows. The goal is to build a tribe of followers who have chosen you as the place they will always go to get certain products or services. Ultimately, your tribe can enjoy the same sense of community we find in small towns—people know each other, like each other, and help each other.

REFLECTION

Developing Your Service Strategy

An important first step is to define the parameters of your community. Who are they? Where are they located? What are they like? Why will they choose your products or services? Two common types of communities are: 1) the "geographical" community where customers are in a specific location and 2) the "niche" community where customers have a particular interest in the products of an industry. Many of the entrepreneurs we met are building geographical communities (Tim Reiman of Whiffle Boy's Pizza and Dave Twombly of Central Coast Disposal). Others are building niche communities (Allen Lim of Skratch Labs and ENVE Composites). Some are building both types of communities. They are selling products to people in their geographical location and to others in their niche outside their physical boundaries (Jeff Wester of Ponderosa Forge and Patrick Hayden of the Kentucky Gun Co.).

The key practices for developing a strong community are the same regardless of the type of community you are creating. The questions below will help you build a strong tribe of raving fans who love your business.

1. What type of community are you building (geographic, niche, or both), and who are the members?
2. Why will this community be attracted to the products or services of your business?
3. What specific strategies will you use to reach and communicate with your community?
4. What do your major competitors do for their customers to provide exceptional service?
5. What are five things you can do to give your customers more than they expect to receive and more than your competitors are providing?

6. If your customers were to create a "Profile of Mind-Boggling Service" for your business from their perspective, what actions do you think it would include?
7. What type of system can you develop and implement to provide "mind-boggling" service to every customer as your business grows?
8. How can you get your customers more involved in your business in order to provide Level 4 service and build an even stronger community?

CHAPTER

9

Pivot to Multiple Revenue Streams

"We feel like there is tremendous opportunity and a lot more growth potential. The baby, in our minds, is still an infant—that entrepreneurial spirit is alive and well. We test markets, and when we get a good bite on that hook, we set it hard. When the water gets rough, we back out, evaluate, and go a different direction. We are focused on opportunity, not clothing or furniture. We will continue to go after emerging markets and grow the business."

—Bill Freedman, cofounder of DownEast Outfitters

If Shawn had not tinkered around in the motorhome for 25 minutes, we would have been five miles past Hazard, Kentucky, when the hard rain hit. If we had left on time, we would not have crossed the rain-soaked railroad tracks just east of town. If we had not crossed the oil-slick tracks, I wouldn't have smacked my head on the asphalt, slashed my elbow, bruised my thigh, or torn the muscles in my groin. And if I hadn't crashed, I could have pedaled across Virginia with two legs rather than one.

On the other hand, if Shawn had not puttered around for nearly half an hour, we would have been five miles outside Hazard without our rain gear when the torrential outburst struck. We might have contracted frostbite, rammed into the back of an Amish horse and buggy, been hit by a truck driver who couldn't see us in the rain, or gotten jumped by an angry troll whose home under a bridge had been washed out. It's funny how a few minutes can dramatically change the trajectory of your life.

We had decided to leave Hazard at 9:00 that morning. As my Type A self, I was ready to go at 8:55. I had donned my riding kit, pulled the bikes off the back of the motorhome, oiled the chains, pumped up the tires, eaten our standard breakfast of granola, yogurt, and chocolate milk, filled my water bottles, and loaded my jersey pockets with gels and bars. We had stayed at a Hampton Inn that night because there was no RV park in the area. When Shawn moseyed out to the bus at 9:00, I knew we had issues. It took him 25 minutes to do the things I had just done. I sat and watched, twiddled my thumbs, and tried not to get too worked up. As we finally mounted our bikes to leave, the rain hit, so we had to go back in the bus to get our waterproof windbreakers, gloves, and warmer socks.

As we were leaving town, a line of cars followed us because there was no shoulder on the narrow road. I picked up the pace to climb a brief rise, and just as I crested the hill . . . BAM! I didn't see the railroad tracks until I was right on top of them. My front tire slid left, and I flew off the bike to the right. I hit the right side of my head, my right elbow, and my right hip—hard. As I lay there in a fog, I heard the siren. My first thought was, "This cannot be happening to me."

Ricky, the driver of a fire and rescue vehicle, was stopped at a crossroad and saw the crash. He thought the woman behind me had run me over. Within seconds his siren was blaring, and he was on the scene. He jumped out of his car and said he would have an ambulance there in a few minutes. *What? Ambulance . . . why?* I had to get off the ground. I stood up, a bit wobbly, and put on my "everything is fine" face.

"Hey, thanks for stopping, but I'm good, no problem." Then I noticed the gathering crowd. The woman following behind us when I crashed was there. Several people behind her had stopped to help. A lady driving the other direction pulled over and joined our circle.

"Are you OK?"

"Do you need help?"

"What can we do?"

To be honest, I didn't know how badly I was hurt, but I didn't want to be the center of a scene in Hazard, Kentucky. Everyone was concerned about letting me go, but I insisted I was fine. My plan was to ride to the next small town and then assess the damage in private. I gingerly mounted my bike and rode at a snail's pace with Shawn following behind. He was cool with whatever I wanted to do, but he kept needling me with questions out of genuine concern: "Are you sure this is a good idea?" "How is your head feeling?" "I know you're a tough guy, but what if you are doing more damage?" I was pretty grumpy and didn't say much. I mumbled: "I'm fine." "Not a problem." "Just keep going." I was trying to stay positive and find my happy place. I had ridden 3,420 miles without a single accident, injury, or close call until now. My mind was made up; I wasn't going to quit.

It took an hour and a half to go 18 miles to the tiny town of Hindman. We pulled into a gas station, and I tried to get off my bike. I couldn't stand on my right leg, and I couldn't swing it over the seat. I eventually laid the bike down, stepped over it, and feigned a cheery mood. The first thing Shawn said was "You have blood all over your hand." Sure enough, I had a nasty gash on my elbow, and blood was flowing down my right arm inside my rain jacket. Shawn rushed into the small convenience store and requisitioned gauze and tape from the clerk's first aid kit. When he returned, he started doing battlefield triage on my various body parts. I had chunks of skin torn off my elbow, a huge bruise the size of a football on my right thigh, pain in my upper hamstring, and torn muscles in my groin. But Shawn was most concerned with my head.

"Who is the president of the United States?" he asked.

"Abraham Lincoln," I replied snidely. "See, I'm fine."

The truth was, my head was woozy, my right leg was in serious pain, and I felt like I had been hit by a northbound train. I still believed I could carry on in some capacity, but I knew I could no longer do what I had been doing for the past 3,420 miles. It was time to pivot to a different game plan.

The Process of Pivoting

I have learned a lot about pivoting from the hundreds of entrepreneurs I have met. One of the great role models I interviewed early on was June Morris, founder of Morris Air. June is the only woman in America to own and operate a major jet airline service. She started her career as a travel agent and worked for American Express. When she married her husband, Mitch, she wanted more freedom to travel with him, so she quit her job. Mitch kept telling her she should start her own travel agency. June didn't believe she could do it, but Mitch was very encouraging, so she started a one-person agency called Morris Travel. With Mitch as her cheerleader, she started hiring people and courting a business clientele. Before long she had dozens of employees and hundreds of accounts with corporations, universities, and government agencies.

After a few years, airlines started selling tickets directly to their own customers, and June was concerned her business might erode. That's when she heard about a 24-year-old kid named Dave Neeleman (the future founder of JetBlue Airways), who had his own Hawaiian vacation business. She partnered with Dave, who now had the support of a large travel agency, and they moved into the leisure travel niche big time (Pivot 1). They negotiated great fares from a number of airlines and created land packages in Hawaii, Florida, and other attractive tourist locations. This partnership was extremely successful, and they were "selling tons of tickets." In fact, they were so successful that they started chartering their own planes rather than booking their customers on the scheduled airlines (Pivot 2). Here is how June explains this change:

> *When you charter an airplane, the airline provides the crew and everything—all you do is buy the tickets. So basically we were a marketing company, marketing the same way we were before, only now we were selling our own product. If we didn't sell the seats, we ate 'em [laughs]. It was just a kick, because we even traded things for seats. We didn't want any vacant. We had motorcycles, drapes, everything you can imagine. But we were profitable right from the*

first. It was a real plus for people to fly to Hawaii for $399 when they'd been paying $800. So it really opened up a huge market for us.

June and Dave grew the charter business quickly. Before long they had thousands of customers flying on hundreds of planes all around the United States. One of the challenges with this business model was they lacked control over the pilots, the flight attendants, the customer service, and other issues that were important to them. They also had problems with some of the planes they chartered from various airlines; they were often late, and one year Braniff Airways went out of business, which left them with thousands of stranded customers. About this time Alaska Airlines filed a complaint against the company, arguing that it was actually a scheduled airline pretending to be a charter company. June's response was, "OK, if that's the way it is going to be, then we are going to be an airline." That's when Morris Air was born (Pivot 3).

Morris Air grew rapidly. Over the next few years, the company leased 24 planes, hired hundreds of pilots and flight attendants, opened a reservation center, and hired several thousand employees. All this growth was funded with cash flow. According to June, "It was just like a little goose laying a golden egg." This is when Herb Kelleher decided Morris Air was a perfect fit with Southwest Airlines. June sold the company for $139 million and joined the board at Southwest. Herb held a hangar party for her attended by several thousand people and rolled out a brand-new Boeing 737 with her name on it—the *June M. Morris*. When June was a little girl, she used to look up into the sky, see a plane, and wonder what it would be like to fly on one. Now little girls around the country see the *June M. Morris* and believe that they, too, can achieve their dreams.

The story of Morris Air is not atypical of entrepreneurial adventures. In fact, it has been the norm with the hundreds of thriving entrepreneurs I have worked with and interviewed. They seldom end up running the company they originally launch. Here is what happens: Successful entrepreneurs discover a true business opportunity, as defined in Chapter 4. Using a variety of resources, they launch a low-cost prototype, as discussed in Chapter 6. They modify their product, service, or business model as needed based on ongoing interaction with their customers. As their venture starts to grow, they see a variety of opportunities, based on their increasing knowledge and experience in the marketplace. They soon discover other true business opportunities that they pivot to in several ways: 1) They find new products for their growing customer base, 2) they find new market niches for their growing product line, and 3) they use their growing resources to develop new products and services for related business opportunities. In other words, they do not remain stagnant. As June Morris explains, "One of the things entrepreneurs need to know is that you can never really stay the same. You have to constantly keep growing; otherwise you are going to shrink." This tendency to diversify within an industry or related industries provides multiple streams of revenue and reduces the vulnerability of a single product or service.

Thus, thriving business founders apply shorter-term planning that is opportunity driven. They continue to amend a "portfolio of products and services" based on feedback from customers, tactics of competitors, new technology, and missing pieces in the marketplace. It's like they are running a test kitchen in tandem with their core business, and there is always something cooking in the kitchen. Sometimes these new opportunities supplement the core business, and other times they become the new core business. The model in Figure 9–1 on page 147 illustrates the various ways successful entrepreneurs pivot to new revenue streams, and thus increase the sustainability of their companies.

Let's discuss the pivots June Morris made in light of this model. June started selling basic travel services to the business community: airline tickets, lodging, ground transportation, etc. (Quadrant 1—base product line to base market). When she felt her core business might start eroding, she began selling the same basic services to leisure travelers (Quadrant 3—base product line to new market). Wanting more control over the flights she was booking, June started her charter airline service. While her leisure travel customers benefited

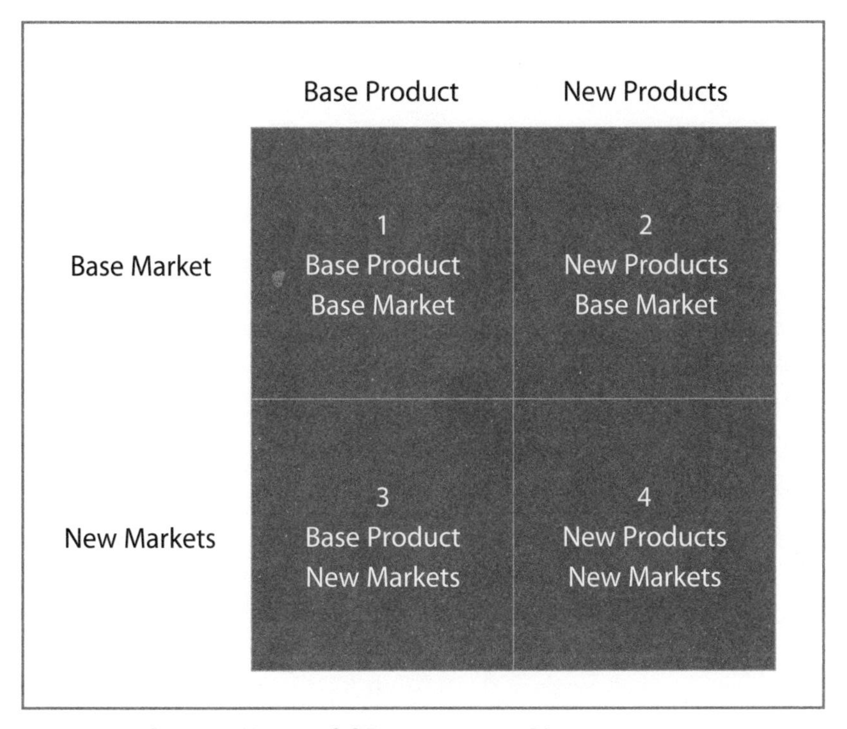

Figure 9–1: **The Ways Successful Entrepreneurs Pivot**

from this shift, she quickly added dozens of charter flights to cities around the country, which opened up many new markets for non-leisure travelers (Quadrant 4—new products to new markets). When June started Morris Air, she fully anchored her business in Quadrant 4. In fact, after starting her airline, she sold Morris Travel to her employees, giving up Quadrants 1 and 3. Morris Air was now her new core business.

Our Pivoting Entrepreneurs

Nearly all the entrepreneurs we met on our ride across America, and others I have interviewed over the years, have made at least one pivot to create additional revenue for their business. Some have made two or three. Let's talk about some of these remarkable role models in light of the four quadrants in the diagram above.

Base Product to Base Market (Quadrant 1)

If you launch a true business opportunity, your chances for success go up dramatically. However, this does not mean you won't need to pivot a bit before you establish your base product in your base market. Feedback from your early customers will help you tweak your product, pricing, packaging, and service system. Sometimes these early shifts can be quite dramatic before you gain traction. For example, Matthew and Kate Maloney created software to help businesses improve their Google rankings. To prove that their model worked, they started selling monk's robes on their platform. Sales were so strong that they pivoted to the online costume business as their new core company. Today, Costume Craze is one of the largest retailers of costumes in the world. In the end, increasing sales is the only indicator of whether your core business is working.

Once you are successfully generating revenue, you need to do everything possible to sell your base product to your base market. You don't pivot to new revenue streams just for the sake of pivoting. I have seen many aspiring entrepreneurs chase everything shiny and never establish a solid business foundation. You only want to pursue additional revenue streams when it makes sense or is necessary to survive. So focus on your core business before you pursue alternative revenue streams.

All the entrepreneurs you have met in this book so far have built strong core businesses selling their basic product line to their base market. Remember Jason Kintzler, founder of Pitchengine in Lander, Wyoming? He created a robust content creation platform to help corporations tell their story through social media. Jason is one of the most talented entrepreneurs I interviewed when it comes to growing his core business. By attending conferences, displaying at trade shows, speaking at universities, aggressively blogging, and working with PR firms, he has added more than 50,000 companies to his platform, including Walmart, PepsiCo, Geico, and Budweiser. In addition, Justin Gold, founder of Justin's, and Allen Lim, founder of Skratch Labs, continue to sell their products to more and more customers in their base market. These talented entrepreneurs are now in a great position to explore other revenue-generating options.

New Products to Base Market (Quadrant 2)

Once you have a community of customers who love your business, you can start thinking of other products for these same buyers. Customers want complete solutions to their pain points, so think about the products they may be purchasing from other businesses in addition to yours to solve their problem. For example, I have worked with two companies in the funeral industry. Obviously, families who lose a loved one need a casket and a funeral service. But they also need flowers, a memory book, a burial plot, and a gravestone. Both the companies I consulted with have added all these services plus various "pre-need" insurance plans so the funeral of the future can be paid for in today's dollars. Customers of these companies only need to make one stop to get everything they need during a difficult time.

Benny and Julie Benson, whom you met in Chapter 2, have created a complete solution for their customers in the alternative energy industry. Initially, they started designing biogas plants that use waste fuels produced at landfills, wastewater treatment plants, and manure storage facilities. After designing a number of these plants, they felt they were in an excellent position to start building them as well, so they added a construction service. Next, they developed an IT solution so they could operate the plants remotely. Now they offer their customers a complete one-stop service that includes designing, building, and operating renewable energy plants—all from their headquarters in Sisters, Oregon.

In addition to adding more products for their base customers, Julie and Benny have also pivoted to Quadrant 4—new products for new markets. While they were building their company, they rented a hangar for their plane at the small airport in Sisters. Because they fly so much, they also rented office space there. Eventually they bought the airport and added additional office space. Now they operate the airport and lease offices to other entrepreneurs in Sisters. Benny and Julie have pivoted their way to the lifestyle of their dreams.

Polly Hinds and Lynda German are also skilled in adding new products for their base customers. They are the founders of Mad Dog and the Pilgrim Booksellers in Sweetwater Station, Wyoming, a town that is 40 miles from the closest store. The two moved to the windswept plains after operating three bookstores and a cleaning service in Denver. One night while they were cleaning a building, a thief ran down the alley and threw his gun in the back of their truck. Within minutes they were face-down on the pavement and being handcuffed by the police. One of the officers gestured at Lynda. "She's got a gun!" he warned.

"No!" shouted Polly. "It's her feather duster!"

It didn't matter. The two were hauled off to jail and released several hours later.

"Have you ever been handcuffed?" Polly asks. "It really hurts."

This bizarre experience of mistaken identity enhanced Lynda and Polly's motivation to leave the big city. They are now masters of doing what they want to do where they want to live. In their hamlet in Sweetwater Station, they have chickens, sheep, peacocks, a donkey, and a llama. They also have 70,000 used and antiquarian books in their barn, which is more than most Barnes & Nobles carry, ranging in price from $10 to $4,000. Although a fourth of their sales occur online, most of their revenue comes from friends, neighbors, loyal customers, and curious visitors. According to Lynda, "We have more walk-in traffic here than we ever had in Denver." To better serve their growing tribe of customers, they also sell soap, fresh eggs, and wool from their 40 Navajo-Churro sheep. This breed of sheep is very hardy in harsh conditions and has two layers of wool that can be woven into heirlooms that will last for generations. Of their bold experiment in community building, Lynda says:

> *What we do in our small circle with our friends and neighbors is what's going to change the world. If you are happy, caring, and giving, and you do that in your small circle, you are as important as any president or any prime minister on the planet. Because you're going to change things in your small circle, and that gets bigger and bigger and bigger.*

These are just a few examples of the ways savvy entrepreneurs create new products for their growing customer base. We saw this happening again and again, all across America. For example, Bill

Bezuk has continued to add more and more products for his customers involved in urban farming. He started with chickens and chicken feed, and then added rabbits, beehives, and various types of coops and shelters. He displays all these items in his store so you can see how they might fit in your backyard. Justin Gold started selling nut butters in jars to his customers. Next he added single-serving squeeze packs, and then organic peanut butter cups. So the important question is, "What else do my customers need that is related to my base product line?" The more you can provide complete solutions for your customers, the better.

Base Product to New Markets (Quadrant 3)

You met Gail and Will Williams, the founders of Idaho Sewing for Sports, in Chapter 2. They moved to northern Idaho to raise their kids in a beautiful environment, started making padded cushions for ski resorts, and now sell to hundreds of resorts all over the world. Over the years, Gail and Will also branched out to additional industries. They now make padding for pole vaulting and high jumping pits, as well as protective padding for the military and law enforcement. For the most part, they will make anything anybody wants that requires padding. Selling their services to a variety of industries has allowed them to fully use their expensive cutting and sewing equipment. Gail and Will's son, Gunther, is now the CEO of the company. Here is how he explains their philosophy:

> *There are not a lot of places that will make whatever you want. You call us up with an issue, you got to pad something or cover something, we make it. It doesn't really matter. We work right with the customer. We turn [the request] into something we can make. . . . It's kind of our niche.*

Becky Anderson has also sold her initial product line to new markets. She first opened a retail bath and body shop to create jobs for her four daughters. Based on customer requests for specific ingredients, they started developing their own product line. One day a manufacturer's rep suggested they start selling their products wholesale; he helped them design their packaging and provided leads to potential customers. Before long they were wholesaling a number of home and personal care products. One of their successful innovations was a line of soy candles. Within a few years, they were the largest privately held manufacturer of soy candles in the country. Becky has since sold that company, For Every Body, and launched a line of similar products in the direct-sales industry. Her great passion is helping other women have the same experience she has had in business. Here is how Becky describes her growth strategy:

> *I have a saying that I call 'Fly to the roosts that make money,' which is going to where the business is going to be. Or, to steal from Wayne Gretzky, 'Go to where the hockey puck is going to be.' Don't get so stuck in your rut that you don't see opportunities. What we are doing today may not be what we are doing tomorrow. We are going to move as quickly as the market does.*

Many of the entrepreneurs we met across America are taking their products to new markets. For example, Patrick Hayden, founder of the Kentucky Gun Co., started selling his guns and accessories in his geographical region. Now he sells his products online to customers across the country. Winfield and Joy Durham, founders of Sisters Coffee Company, have opened additional retail locations in Oregon but are also wholesaling their coffee in ten states around the West. Winfield has sold accounts in places he likes to go fishing. The important question here is simple: "What other customer niches might want my products or services?" There are always new places you can go.

New Products to New Markets (Quadrant 4)

Adam Hepworth, Jared Richards, and Dan Nebeker lived in a blue house while attending college. They also spent a lot of time on the ski slopes. When they graduated, they decided to create a company called Bluehouse Skis. Adam's dad asked me to talk to him about this crazy venture, and after our meeting, I was pretty sure the business could work. They had designed a special ski for skiing powder, their great passion, and planned to order 500 pairs of these skis from China and sell them to friends, relatives, and powder enthusiasts online. The worst-case scenario was that they would have to sell the skis at cost to get their investment back. It seemed like a pretty low-risk experiment to me.

Over the next few years they worked hard to build a successful company. But the ski industry is capital-intensive with low margins, so making money was a challenge. During this time, Adam's wife and her two sisters would get their nails done during their "Sisters' Day Out." They loved the outing, but it was expensive and difficult to keep their nails looking good for more than a week. Then they had an epiphany: Bluehouse Skis had a laminating machine to put graphics on skis, so why not create stick-on fingernails that would last three or four weeks? They could create a plethora of unique designs that would be much less expensive than going to the nail salon. So Jamberry Nails was born, using the resources of the existing company, and became the new priority. Today, Jamberry Nails has more than 100,000 distributors who demonstrate and sell the product line. During our bike ride across America, we met a handful of exuberant ladies who sell Jamberry Nails. They are doing the same thing the Bluehouse team did when they created Jamberry: building additional revenue for themselves in tandem with their existing jobs or businesses—new products in a new market.

One of the most fascinating entrepreneurs we met on our journey is Joe Brandl, owner of Absaroka Western Designs & Tannery, located on the eastern slopes of the Teton Mountains in the town of Dubois, Wyoming, population 995. We crested the snow-covered Continental Divide at 9,658 feet and sped down the mountain on our bikes to meet Joe at this showroom at 6,946 feet. Joe received a degree in natural resources from the University of Nebraska and took a job with the Wyoming Game and Fish Department. Here is why he has stayed in Dubois for nearly 30 years:

> *When we first moved to town, nobody knew us, and then my wife got cancer. The people in the town came through and did everything for us. We had hospital bills that were tremendous and didn't have*

> *a dime for anything. People would come by and stick money in my pockets. Things like that constantly happen here. It doesn't matter what your political background is, when it hits the fan, people come together miraculously. So I live in Dubois because of the community that's here.*

While working for Game and Fish, Joe took a part-time job at a small tannery in town. He later bought the business. Over the years, he has tanned hides for people in all 50 states, everything from "mice to moose." His customers are taxidermists, hunters, wildlife departments, zoos, lodges, and cabin owners. Along the way, people started asking Joe if he could make clothing and props for mountain man rendezvous, sportsmen's shows, and movies. Joe always says yes and has now created customized products for hundreds of projects, including movies like *Dances with Wolves*, *The Last of the Mohicans*, and *Wind River*.

As Joe continued to receive requests for western products, he decided to open his own showroom in Dubois to feature the variety of things he can design and make. His showroom is a spectacular, lodge-like setting. Walking through it is an adventure in history. It displays lodge pole beds, tables, chairs, wall hangings, rawhide lampshades, antler cabinet knobs, blankets, wildlife pictures, teepees, painted buffalo skulls, animal-skin robes, moose-hide Christmas stockings, and a stuffed lion. Joe also carries his new line of pet chews he makes from leftover rawhide. When asked to summarize his business philosophy, Joe replies:

> *I like to think of myself as a renaissance man, and I like to think of the business as a renaissance business. I dabble in a lot of different things, anything from building you a lodge pole bed to the buffalo hide that goes on it to the drum that you beat at night in the teepee that I built for you. I can do all of those things. So I try to diversify as much as possible. My next step is to teach outdoor education and outdoor survival.*

I have dozens of stories about entrepreneurs like Joe who use their resources to create new products for new markets. For example, Randy Hamann is the founder of Weingarten Vineyard in Ste. Genevieve,

Missouri. He bought a beautiful piece of property and started growing grapes and making wine. He then built an upscale winery. To better take advantage of his land and building, he added a restaurant, gift shop, and art gallery. He also holds weddings and corporate events on his property. Over the years, he has created a destination business that caters to a variety of customer niches. Jeff Wester, whom you met in Chapter 6, built an old-fashioned blacksmith shop and eventually created more than 100 new products to sell to customers online. We met Dennis and Jenny Sykora while they were on a job in Kansas. They harvest soybeans and corn on their farm in Minnesota every fall, but during the spring and summer, they harvest other farmers' crops in the Midwest. The key is to inventory your growing resources and consider what else you can do with them. This is creative rather than linear logic. Don't think, "I want to build "A" so I need to go get the resources." Rather think, "I have all these resources, how can I fully utilize them?"

Winning entrepreneurs continue to seek out and develop multiple streams of revenue. They do this by offering related products to their growing customer base, finding new markets for their growing product line, and creating new ventures with their growing resources. Over time, they end up juggling a reasonable number of projects in the same or related industries. This is why most successful entrepreneurs end up building a different company than they originally envisioned. They pursue emerging opportunities that they didn't know existed when they started. By pivoting to multiple revenue streams, you reduce the vulnerability of a narrow product line, alter your business with changing market conditions, and create long-term stability for your enterprise.

My Pivot to a New Strategy

So there we were at the gas station in tiny Hindman, Kentucky. I was all patched up and wondering what to do next. I called Mary, who was driving the motorhome that day. She and Jay were still back in Hazard, doing laundry and editing video. It would take them several hours to get to us. So rather than sit around suffering, I decided I would continue to limp along at the speed of molasses in January and see how far I could go. I ended up riding 70 miles that day. It was raining, cold, and painful. We stopped at a hotel that night to reassess the damage. As I drifted into a fitful sleep, I knew I would be worse in the morning. And I was right.

"You can't ride your bike anymore!"

We were sitting in the lobby of the hotel, and Mary was being awfully firm.

"Remember when Lance Armstrong got testicular cancer?" I replied.

Mary started to laugh. "You're unbelievable!"

"I'm not saying I'm Lance Armstrong, especially since he confessed to doping his whole career," I said. "What I am saying is that all his doctors told him he would never ride again, so he found a doctor who was willing to help him get back on his bike."

Mary rolled her eyes. "I'm listening."

"That's what I need right now. I don't need you to tell me all the reasons I can't ride; I need you to help me figure out how to get back on my bike."

"OK, what do you want to do?"

I thought of the movie *Gravity*, where Sandra Bullock is drifting in space, losing all hope of being rescued. George Clooney appears to her in a dream and says, "There is always something you can do." So I started brainstorming with myself. My first plan was to buy a long bungee cord and connect it from my handlebars to the back of Shawn's bike. He has a big motor, but I was pretty sure he wouldn't go for that. Then I called my good friend Margo Brady, who owns a physical therapy practice in Salt Lake City. She has nursed me through running, biking, and water-skiing injuries over the years. She assured me I could ride if I slowed down and put minimal pressure on my right leg. In fact, she said, the increased blood flow at a low level of intensity could help the healing process. She also recommended medication for infections, swelling, and pain.

Fortunately, I had gone to see my favorite doctor, Russ Toronto, prior to our excursion. He strongly suggested I pick up several prescriptions in case of emergencies. "You don't want to have an accident and have to go find a clinic," he told me. I had taken his advice and already had a small pharmacy in the motorhome: Cipro for infections, diclofenac for inflammation, and hydrocodone for pain. So I pivoted to a new strategy that matched the resources I had with the challenges that lay ahead. I started taking Cipro and diclofenac immediately. We shortened our rides for the next few days, riding at 14 to 15 miles an hour rather than 18 to 20. I only pedaled with my left leg for three days, and I took the hydrocodone at the end of each ride—I didn't want to take it during the day, go loopy, and crash again.

This new strategy worked great. After three days I could push down on my right pedal. After five days, I could push down, pull up, and thrust forward. I could even climb big mountains again, which was fantastic, because we rode through the Appalachians and climbed up to the Blue Ridge Parkway in Virginia. From the small town of Vesuvius, we climbed 2,000 feet in four miles with grades of 12 to 22 percent. It was a killer but well worth the suffering, with some of the most spectacular scenery I have ever seen. By the last three days across Virginia, I was almost back to normal. My crash turned out to be a positive experience, one I will never forget.

Entrepreneurship, like life itself, is all about recovery. It isn't about falling down, making poor choices, or doing silly things. It is about getting back up, creating new plans, soldiering onward, and learning valuable lessons that make us stronger. Most of the entrepreneurs I have met have had their "crash in Hazard." They are successful today because they got back up, changed course, and kept on riding. Learning to pivot, sometimes out of necessity and sometimes for sound diversification reasons, is one of the greatest tools you have for building a thriving enterprise and achieving your dreams.

REFLECTION

Planning Your Pivots

The best time to think about pivoting is long before you actually do it. I encourage all the aspiring entrepreneurs I advise to contemplate what they will do if their initial product does not gain traction. I also encourage existing business owners to consider pivots they can make to generate additional revenue streams to solidify their business. In the end, you want a portfolio of products and services that reduces your vulnerability and increases long-term sustainability. The strategy outlined below can help you successfully plan your pivots to new opportunities.

1. Define the broader problem people are trying to solve when they purchase your product.
2. List other related products your customers may be buying elsewhere to fully solve this problem.
3. Ask your customers which of these products they might be more likely to buy from you if the quality is great and the price is right.
4. Create an action plan to start developing and testing the highest-ranked product on the list with your base customers.
5. Brainstorm additional customer niches that may be interested in your base product.
6. Find an initial customer to partner with so you can test the viability of your product in one of these new markets.
7. Inventory all the resources you have and determine how you might use them in related ventures without incurring significant startup costs.
8. Assemble a brain trust of advisors to help you evaluate, develop, and implement a test of one of these new opportunities in a new market.

CHAPTER

10

Serve Your Broader Community

"Our bottom line is the utilization of profits to enrich the human soul and alleviate human suffering. We always try to combine a humanitarian project that will genuinely help the people with our business interests. Until we move beyond the profit level and help find cures for cancer, provide for the homeless, and feed the poor, we haven't achieved our corporate objectives."

—Jon Huntsman Sr., founder of Huntsman Corporation

Mission accomplished: 4,000 miles, 45 days, 100 remarkable entrepreneurs. It is hard to describe the emotions of accomplishing a once-unimaginable dream, but we did it with purpose, zealous tenacity, resourcefulness, and teamwork. Finishing this feat at the *Monument to the Alliance and Victory* above the beach in Yorktown is the ultimate capstone experience. On October 17, 1781, after six years of fighting, a red-coated British drummer mounted a parapet and beat out the call for a parley. When the firing stopped, a British officer waving a white handkerchief approached the American lines. He was blindfolded and taken to General George Washington to negotiate the terms of surrender. At 2 P.M. on October 19, British General Charles O'Hara formally surrendered his sword to the Americans on behalf of

Lord Cornwallis, who claimed to be ill that day. It was the beginning of a new nation founded upon the principles of individual freedom, self-government, and citizen problem solving.

Following the end of the Revolutionary War, our forefathers and foremothers enthusiastically implemented our grand experiment in freedom. They worked together to build each other's barns and plant each other's crops; they built businesses and learned various trades to meet the needs of their communities; they held town meetings to plan their schools, roads, and cities; they cared for the sick and afflicted and adopted the children of those who had tragically passed away. It was a remarkable display of "all for one and one for all."

Eyes from abroad watched this experiment in freedom with great interest and curiosity. The ruling nobles were sure it would fail. The common citizens hoped it would prevail and set a precedent for the world. In 1831, Alexis de Tocqueville, a French political philosopher, came to America to examine our attempt at self-rule and citizen problem solving up close. He published his observations in a two-volume work entitled *Democracy in America*. De Tocqueville concluded that the essence of this new society took place in our small communities—just like the ones we visited:

> *When an American seeks the cooperation of his fellows, they seldom refuse him, and I have often noticed that their help is both spontaneous and enthusiastic. Should some unforeseen accident occur on the public highway, people run from all sides to help the victim; should some family fall foul of an unexpected disaster, a thousand strangers willingly open their purses and a goodly number of modest gifts come to aid their distress. Frequently among the most civilized nations of the world, a poor wretch happens to find himself as isolated at the heart of a crowd as a savage in his own woods; such a thing is almost never seen in the United States.*

We witnessed this same spirit of community that Alexis de Tocqueville observed during our ride across America. The successes we have seen would not be possible in many parts of the world, where citizen problem solving is not allowed or encouraged. Sure, we have our challenges, because we are a nation of humans run by humans. The beauty of America, though, is that we get to participate in coming up with the solutions. One of the best ways to do this is through the organizations we create. The role models in this book are not only building their own dreams but also making significant contributions to the communities they serve, just as de Tocqueville observed nearly 200 years ago.

Business as a Format for Problem Solving

One of my most memorable trips to the airport was to pick up Mimi Silbert and three of her residents from the Delancey Street Foundation in San Francisco. I had spoken with Mimi on the phone at length a few years before but had never met her in person. I knew what she looked like, but I didn't know who she was bringing with her. When Mimi came down the stairs to baggage claim, she was followed by what looked like three corporate executives: very well groomed, expensive wool suits, white shirts, and nice leather shoes. I later learned that James ran the Delancey Street construction company, Michael worked in the food service business, and Stephanie was Mimi's assistant. No one at the airport would ever have guessed that all three had spent many years in prison.

Mimi grew up in an immigrant ghetto in Boston. Her grandparents, parents, uncles, and aunts all lived together in very close quarters, supported each other, and worked together to achieve the American Dream. Eventually, they all moved upward and onward, but they remained very close. Their extended family support system helped them succeed. In fact, it worked so well that Mimi eventually earned two master's degrees and two Ph.D.s.

Early in her career, Mimi taught criminology and psychology at the University of California, Berkeley, in addition to working as a prison psychologist. She was frustrated that so many convicts ended up right back in prison shortly after they were released. She felt that what was missing was the extended family support that she had had growing up. These convicts didn't have a clue how to make it in America. It was like they were from a foreign country and had to "learn a whole new culture for living successfully." Excited to put her extended-family concept into practice, she and 15 ex-convicts moved into the former Russian Consulate in Pacific Heights, one of the most prestigious neighborhoods in San Francisco. Mimi explains her rationale:

> *It really was a perfect neighborhood for us because we wanted our people to become everything these neighbors were. Unfortunately, the neighborhood went completely crazy. Everyone thought crime would go up and property values would go down. We decided to show them we would be the best neighbors possible, even though we were ex-cons and ex-drug addicts.*

A theme Mimi repeated a lot in those early days was, "You can't cure an alcoholic in a bar." To show the neighbors they were good citizens who could contribute to the neighborhood, they volunteered their services to anyone who needed help. One day some neighbors asked them to help clear out their home because they were having a benefit for the ballet and needed the furniture moved into the garage so there would be more standing room in the house. As Mimi was directing the project, one of her guys picked up a piano and said, "Uh, Mimi, whatta you want me to do with this?" Mimi said a light went on inside her head and she thought, "That's it! These guys have been pumping iron in prison for years, so they could come to Delancey Street and start a moving company."

That very day they went back home and made fliers that said, "MOVING? WE WILL DO IT FOR LESS!" They circulated them throughout the area, and people started calling. They called other moving companies and got quotes to figure out pricing and then rented uniforms and a Hertz truck. This was the beginning of what would become one of the most successful moving companies in California: Delancey Street Movers. When I visited Mimi in San Francisco, the company had dozens of trucks and a number of big diesel rigs. Today, Delancey Street Movers is one of more than 20 businesses Mimi and her residents have started as part of the rehabilitation process. They own and operate a construction company, a printing business, restaurants, a bookstore, an auto repair shop, a furniture-making company, and others. Mimi explains how they do it:

> *Each of these training schools/businesses is started with that entrepreneurial spirit. We always say, 'Okay, we need money to stay alive, and there's an opportunity here. We just need to learn how to do this, and then do it better than anyone else.' So we jump in, work hard, and usually come out winners!*

The best example of their "jump in and figure it out" attitude is the 400,000-square-foot complex they built on the waterfront on Embarcadero Street in San Francisco. Mimi became a general contractor, obtained a $4 million unsecured loan from Bank of America, built the facility with 350 ex-convicts, and in just three years paid the loan back in full from their revenues. They also have facilities in Los Angeles, New York, New Mexico, North Carolina, and South Carolina. All their businesses and facilities are self-sustaining. They don't take any money from the government, so their programs are not funded by taxpayers.

Here is how the most successful rehabilitation program in the world works. People come to Delancey Street either on their own or through the judicial system. They are typically ex-convicts, drug addicts, or homeless individuals. Other programs would not take a lot of these people, so Delancey Street is the court of last resort. Mimi explains:

> *I always tell people we are the Harvard of the underclass. Just like Harvard takes the top 2 percent, we take the bottom 2 percent. But our people leave with the academics, three marketable career skills, and lots of survival and interpersonal skills. So I think we are better than Harvard. I know we have a better football team [laughs].*

When residents arrive at Delancey Street, they are put in a "minion" or family of ten people. They are responsible for themselves and each other. They learn about hygiene and interpersonal relationships and start to work in one of the companies, where they are mentored by the person who held that job before them. It's an "each one teach one" mentoring program. There are no professional staff members—no psychiatrists, psychologists, or social workers. Residents continue to progress to higher levels of leadership in their first company, and then move to another company. They do this until they have developed three marketable career skills. It generally takes four years for each resident to gain the experience required to make it in the real world, and more than 90 percent of them do. They don't go back to drugs or prison; instead, they are working as lawyers, medical professionals, contractors, business owners, and even law enforcement officers. Thousands of men and women who hit bottom in life have graduated from Delancey Street and are now happy and productive citizens—and great neighbors.

Mimi Silbert was one of the first to show me the remarkable power of business as a format for changing the world. You probably noticed that she follows the key principles for entrepreneurial success presented in this book: She has a powerful purpose, relies on her past experiences, launches true opportunities, develops teams, maximizes her resources (an unlimited supply of ex-cons), works with zealous tenacity, builds communities of raving fans, pivots to multiple revenue streams, and benefits the broader community. Mimi is a superb example of how creating businesses can not only help us achieve our own dreams, but can also benefit the lives of other people far more effectively than many government-run programs.

When I started my career, there was a clear distinction between nonprofit organizations and for-profit businesses. Nonprofit managers were big-hearted people who often lacked or even shunned business practices. Business owners and corporate executives were often only interested in making money. Today, the lines are much more blurred, as savvy leaders are using entrepreneurial practices to address serious problems in our communities. This exciting movement is happening through a variety of organizational formats, both for-profit and nonprofit. There are owners of large corporations donating their profits to worthy causes. There are entrepreneurs creating for-profit companies that address social issues like education, literacy, the environment, and health care. There are business owners spinning off nonprofit organizations that solve problems related to their industry. And there are leaders like Mimi Silbert creating enterprising nonprofits that use business concepts to change people's lives. I consider all these people "social entrepreneurs," a term I define broadly as anyone who conceives, creates, manages, and assumes the risk of an enterprise created for the good of society.

When I started collecting stories from successful entrepreneurs more than 20 years ago, I expected to find certain common practices, like maximizing resources, building strong teams, and so on. What I did not expect to find was a strong passion for serving the broader community. The story I heard frequently went like this: "I had no idea we would be this successful. It's really our customers who got us where we are today. I would really like to do something for this community." What the community said in turn was: "This business supports us, so let's support this business." So serving the community helped strengthen these businesses, even though this was not their original goal. The fact is, being intimately involved in the fabric of your community helps you build your tribe of raving fans, which we discussed in Chapter 8. When you serve the same community that is buying your products or services, the impact on your brand reputation can be significant. Your giving, though, must be authentic and flow naturally from your purpose of being in business in the first place. You must have a genuine passion for making a difference in the lives of others.

Our Big-Hearted Entrepreneurs

The entrepreneurs we met across America are heavily involved in serving their communities, even more so than other groups I have interviewed. They are supporting schools, mentoring students, raising money for health care, sharing their resources, sponsoring teams and clubs, creating jobs, and providing for the needy. I could tell dozens of stories about the ways these entrepreneurs are making meaningful contributions in their communities. Here are just a few examples.

Benny and Julie Benson

Benny and Julie, the founders of Energyneering Solutions in Sisters, Oregon, believe schools are the heart of any community. As a result, they are heavily involved in their local schools in a number of ways. As engineers, they help design and teach classes in science, technology, engineering, math, aviation, and meteorology. Their hope is to light a spark in students to explore careers in these fields. Each summer they hire between six and ten student interns to work for them. While serving on the school district's budget review committee, Julie realized how much they were spending on heat. This was a problem Energyneering Solutions was well-equipped to solve. The company designed, built, and now operates a biomass plant for the high school, which saves the school tens of thousands of dollars a year.

Gail, Will, and Gunther Williams

As you learned in Chapter 2, Gail, Will, and Gunther Williams believe the purpose of their business, Idaho Sewing for Sports, is to create jobs for people who need employment, and then to bless their lives. During the last recession, work slowed down, and they were faced with the heart-rending decision of whether to lay people off. They figured they had about 20 hours of work each week per employee, so after a great deal of thought and prayer, they decided to ask employees to work 20 hours a week in the business and 20 hours in the community. The company would continue to pay everyone who chose to participate for a 40-hour work week. The employees were thrilled. They each wrote the names of people and organizations that needed help on a large whiteboard, and when they finished their work at the company each week, they would go out and participate in the community projects listed: cutting wood, roofing homes, and caring for the elderly. According to Gail, "Sometimes we didn't have the money in the bank, and it would come right down to the wire, and then a job would come through the door that we could do quickly and collect the money." The company was able to meet payroll every week until the economy improved. The governor of Idaho later gave the company an award for this amazing program.

Mary DeLima

One year Mary's business was a bit slow at DeLima Stables in Harrodsburg, Kentucky. She had a lot of craft supplies that hadn't been used, so she decided to run a camp for disabled and disadvantaged children. She went to the local school board and got the names of 20 children who were receiving financial assistance and did not have money for extracurricular activities, and she and a group of volunteers created a camp for them. They learned how to ride and care for horses and participated in various crafts. Mary, her volunteers, and the kids had a remarkable bonding experience. A group of Mary's customers were so impressed with the program that they helped her establish a nonprofit organization called On the Wings of Horses. Today, the school board recommends local children for the program every fall. After five evening sessions, the children who are most interested can continue all year. Along with riding skills, the program teaches responsibility and respect for others, and has a large impact on the children's lives.

ENVE Composites

When Paul and Sarah Lehman moved to Ogden, Utah, to help Brett and Taylor Satterthwaite build their business, Sarah told Paul she would stay one year, and then she was going back to New York. That was more than ten years ago. Sarah explains:

> *I can't imagine living anywhere else. I absolutely love the fact that ENVE is based in Ogden. The value of being in a small town is that we have the whole community behind us. I feel like we are surrounded by people who are cheering us on. How awesome is that? They bring us into community events and also make us aware of things that are relevant to our business. . . . It's walking down the street in your ENVE shirt and having people say, 'Hey, ENVE, rock on!' You don't get that in a big city.*

Due to their love for the city, the ENVE team is heavily involved in local activities that are relevant to their business. They support biking events and local trails and are working with the mayor to create more bike lanes. One year, Brett and Taylor's bike shop hired a trail crew to pull weeds and groom trails throughout the area. The ENVE team strongly believes that supporting cycling can make the community it loves even better.

Patrick Hayden

Serving the broader community is a significant part of Patrick's business. As owner of the Kentucky Gun Co., he supports hunters' safety courses, 4-H shooting sports, National Guard programs, and a variety of fundraisers in the community. One year a local police officer was killed in the line of duty; Patrick helped raise $62,000 through an auction and donated all the funds to the officer's family. Approximately 90 percent of the donations came from his online community. Patrick believes activities like this are important "because it shows our customers that we're not just here to sell them something."

Richard Chaves

Richard is one of the most community-focused entrepreneurs we met during our trip across the country. He is the founder of Chaves Consulting in Baker City, Oregon. You have already met his son Ryan and his daughter-in-law Kaylin, the founders of Kicks Sportswear. Richard's grandparents had tickets to come to America on the *Titanic.* At the last minute they sold their tickets because they didn't feel their clothes were fancy enough to travel in such luxury. They sailed on another ship and eventually settled in the Baker Valley region of eastern Oregon. Richard's father grew up in the area and owned a grocery store for more than 20 years. When Richard graduated from college, he took a job at the courthouse with the Baker County government. For several years he handled the budget, accounts payable, payroll, and child support and was the chief elections deputy. This is where Richard learned about the business side of government.

The county eventually purchased an IBM computer, and Richard became the data processing manager. At the time, there were very few software programs for cities and counties, so Richard wrote his own. After doing this for five years, he launched his own business. Initially, Chaves Consulting developed software for government organizations, primarily small- to medium-size cities. Richard quickly realized this business was highly dependent on programmers who were expensive, preferred large cities, and moved around every few years. He wondered what kinds of jobs he could create for his friends and neighbors in Baker City. That's when he pivoted to software support, a customer service center, and a large data center for records management. Based on the hiring model presented in Chapter 5, Richard could now hire from Quadrant 2—decent people who could quickly learn the required skills. Today, Chaves Consulting is a multimillion-dollar business that has created hundreds of jobs. Most of the company's projects come through strategic partnerships with organizations that obtain large contracts and then use Richard's business for its unique expertise, whether it is customer service, records management, software support, or elections management. Here is Richard's philosophy for hiring and taking on projects:

> *I'm at a point in my career where making a difference in the community is the most important thing. If somebody comes to me today and says, 'You can have ten new employees and make $50,000 profit next year or you can have a hundred new employees and make $50,000 profit next year,' I would choose the hundred employees because it benefits the community. Here in Baker City a dollar gets spent eight times before it goes back out. So if we bring in $4 million and it gets spent eight times, that's a $32 million difference, which is a big thing for Baker.*

The company's community involvement goes way beyond providing jobs. Richard and his wife, Kathleen, the CEO of the company, have been involved in two major projects in the city. First, they helped raise funds for a 28-acre sports complex, complete with baseball fields, soccer fields, tennis courts, batting cages, and classrooms. Second, they raised $2 million to convert an old Carnegie Library into the Carnegie Art Center, which has studios for artists, a gallery, and classrooms for arts education. For this effort, Chaves Consulting received a Business Committee for the Arts 10 Award in 2012 from Americans for the

Arts "for their exceptional involvement with the arts that enrich the workplace, education, and the community." This remarkable small-town company is now in the same league with Boeing, Bank of America, Microsoft, U.S. Bank, Hallmark Cards, and other large corporations that have received this award—evidence that a small group of passionate people can make a huge difference in their community.

Benefits of Serving Your Community

Entrepreneurs who serve their broader community talk about the extraordinary outcomes it produces. The four outcomes I hear the most often are: 1) it assists the receiver, 2) it transforms the giver, 3) it energizes the organization, and 4) it renews the community. Let's discuss each of these in more detail.

Benefits to the Receiver

The benefits to the receiver are obvious. Students are receiving mentoring, high-risk children are learning new skills, teenagers who were going nowhere are now going to college, people with illnesses are receiving treatment, adults with physical disabilities are finding employment, homeless individuals are locating shelter, people raised in poverty are becoming self-sufficient, and on and on. Many generous business founders are significantly blessing the lives of the people in their communities.

Even more fundamental than the assistance provided is the life-altering transformation many receivers experience when they are served by entrepreneurs who have both compassion and vision. Some people need a whole new orientation to themselves and to life to succeed. Fortunately, humans are malleable enough to make life-altering changes when shown genuine compassion and taught essential life skills. Hence, we see students raised in poverty earning college degrees, addicts freeing themselves from their vices, the needy becoming self-sufficient, and ex-criminals successfully integrating themselves into society. These people are miraculously redeemed from lives of struggle and heartache by generous givers.

Benefits to the Giver

Equally profound is the impact of giving on the giver. Simply put, caring about others to the point of taking action substantially improves the quality of our own lives. As Mimi Silbert constantly teaches her residents at Delancey Street, helping others is the best way to help ourselves. She argues that when person A helps person B, person A gets better; when person B helps person C, person B gets better, and so on. In Christianity it is called the law of the harvest: We reap what we sow. In Eastern religions it's called the law of karma: Present actions determine future destinies. In the vernacular of the street, we say: "What goes around comes around." Our actions set up a chain reaction of events that eventually come back to us in some form. Ultimately, we learn that we have value and are able to contribute to the world, which gives our lives meaning.

I love the story told by Milton Erickson, an icon in the field of short-term therapy, about the power of service as a natural remedy for improving our lives. One of his patients had an aunt in Milwaukee who was despondent. She was 52 years old, independently wealthy, had never married, lived alone, and had no friends. She read the Bible every day and attended her church religiously, but she would slip out at the end of the service, never speaking to anyone. Erickson agreed to visit the woman on his next trip to Milwaukee. When he got to her home, he noticed three large African violets in full bloom in her sunroom; he knew that African violets, though beautiful, are delicate plants that quickly die if neglected. He told the woman he had some medical instructions that would help her get better if she followed them, and she listlessly agreed to do whatever he asked.

Erickson told the woman to go to a nursery and buy 200 African violets of all different hues and take good care of them. Then she was to give an African violet to every couple that got married in her church, every family that had a baby, everyone who got sick, and every family that experienced a death. He also told her to donate African violets to every bazaar held at the church. The woman became known as the "African Violet Queen of Milwaukee" and had many friends of all ages. She died in her 70s, having stayed happy and productive for more than

20 years. So many people attended her funeral that they could not all fit in the church. This incredible transformation took place after just one visit from Erickson, with no probing into the woman's past or insight about her personality. She simply found a worthwhile cause to occupy her attention and link her to people in need.

And so it is that giving can transform the giver. When we are absorbed in our own challenges and activities, we experience a full range of human emotions: anger, fear, elation, depression, joy, and anxiety. When we focus our attention on others, the primary emotion we cultivate is compassion. As we continue to serve, expecting nothing in return, our capacity to care grows to include many individuals, regardless of their circumstances. The entrepreneurs I have met over the years who serve others regularly make new friends, develop new skills, enhance their leadership abilities, increase their professional contacts, and feel more satisfied with their lives.

Benefits to the Organization

Serving your broader community can have a positive impact on your organization. As mentioned above, it provides a great deal of personal fulfillment for team members who participate, which can increase energy, motivation, and morale within your business. Since many people want to work for a company that is making a difference, it can also help you attract partners and team members who share your values. As we discussed in Chapter 2, the new Millennial generation is particularly interested in social responsibility, company values, and service to the community. Companies that serve a broader purpose may have a real advantage attracting this up-and-coming workforce.

Contributing to your community can also improve the overall success of your organization. If you are supporting the community and consequently the community is supporting your business, you will build a large base of loyal customers. Just being big-hearted, though, is not enough to endear people to your organization. You also have to do all the other things successful entrepreneurs do well: Build on your experiences, launch true opportunities, build a strong supporting cast, maximize resources, and give superb customer service. In other words, people will not buy your products or services just because you are doing good things in the community; you also have to run a successful and sustainable business, which means applying the practices we are reviewing in this book.

Benefits to the Community

The fourth outcome of serving the broader community is the impact on the community itself. Obviously, giving can benefit all communities, at least indirectly. You have seen how Benny and Julie Benson built a biomass power plant for their high school; Mary DeLima offers free programs to children from low-income families; ENVE Composites supports biking events and local trails; and Richard and Kathleen Chaves have helped build a sports complex and an arts center. Perhaps most important, building a business creates jobs in a community. As Richard Chaves explained above, each dollar brought into his city is spent eight times before it leaves. This has a positive impact on city revenues and other businesses in the area. Obviously, communities are stronger when organizations are committed to the well-being of their customers and the cities in which they reside.

A Strategy for Serving Your Community

Corporate social responsibility (CSR) has become a hot topic in the business world. Companies of all sizes are being encouraged (and sometimes forced) to become more responsible in their communities. Being a responsible "corporate citizen" includes two important components: 1) things an organization does *to* society, and 2) things an organization does *for* society.

The first component of CSR requires companies to *do no harm* to the communities in which they operate. It is not acceptable to pollute the environment, sell unsafe products, promote unhealthy practices, or mistreat employees. In our new world of social transparency, organizations that do harm in any way will not survive. While this first component of CSR is a *responsibility* of all organizations, the second component is an *opportunity*. In other words, organizations have the basic responsibility to do no harm, but they also have the opportunity to

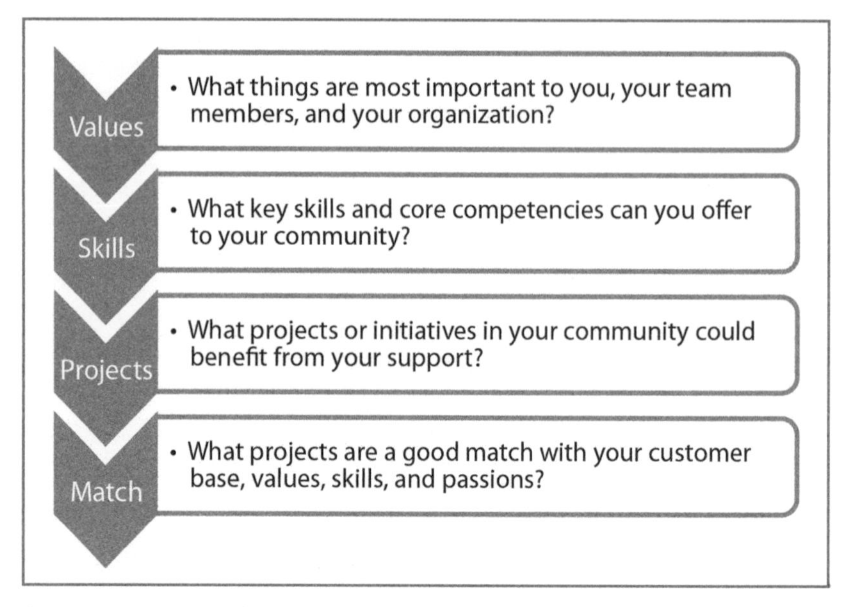

Figure 10–1: **Process for Community Involvement**

make a difference in their communities. Based on our discussion above, there are huge advantages to building an organization that does much more than just make money. The entrepreneurs we met across America are passionate about serving their communities and feel the benefits of doing so far outweigh the effort, time, and cost.

Having worked with hundreds of entrepreneurs who are making significant contributions to their communities, I have observed a simple process they follow for getting involved. This process is illustrated in Figure 10–1.

Clarifying Your Values

Your "why" or purpose for being in business is the foundation for everything you do. Having a clear purpose naturally leads to a set of related values. For example, Richard Chaves's driving purpose is to create jobs in a city he loves. Consequently, he values projects that lead to more jobs. He also values excellent training, ongoing education, and community building. Benny and Julie Benson created their business to maintain a better lifestyle and develop new energy sources. Developing alternative energy requires training in science and technology—thus they value courses in the STEM fields: science, technology, engineering, and mathematics.

Based on your purpose, what are the things you and your teammates value most? Do you value education, continuous learning, innovation, exceptional service, technology development, health and wellness, teamwork, or ethics and integrity? Clarifying your values is an important first step in linking your business with your community. You want to support initiatives that are consistent with your purpose and values, while avoiding things that are not consistent with your purpose and values. Your community involvement should always enhance your overall company brand and reputation.

Assessing Your Skills

After clarifying your company values, the next step is to reflect on the key skills and core competencies of your organization. What are you really good at? What do you do better than other companies? What things can you contribute that other people cannot? Looking at this list, which ones are you the most passionate about? For example, you may be great at calculating your taxes but not very excited about this skill. On the other hand, you may be very good at and very enthusiastic about solving technical problems. The key is to list your core competencies that you are most passionate about sharing. So what are you most interested in? What kinds of activities bring you the most joy? What contributions do you want to make? After answering these questions, you will be ready to identify potential community projects or organizations you want to support.

Finding Potential Projects

As your business grows, many people will approach you about supporting their initiatives. It's great if you can help them, but it's better to select potential projects in advance based on your purpose, values, skills, and passion. Otherwise, you will end up with a hodgepodge of projects that aren't directly related to your brand or community of customers. Creating a list of potential projects is easy: Do a Google search on nonprofits, charities, and social organizations in your area. Many cities also have a nonprofit association that can help identify community needs, or you can call various government agencies and ask which organizations are working on certain problems that interest you: education, human services, workforce services, or rehabilitation. To find the best matches, start with a broad list of projects before narrowing down your options.

Selecting the Best Matches

Now you need to select one or more projects to support that are great matches with your overall company brand, including purpose, values, skills, and passion. I recommend you work with organizations that serve the same community you do. For example, our customers in the food business were interested in health, nutrition, and fitness. Consequently, we supported running events, fitness fairs, and athletic teams. If you are in the food industry, you might support various hunger organizations. If you are in construction, you might get involved in housing projects. If you are in computer services, you might support a school computer literacy program. While serving constituencies outside your community is admirable, it doesn't help you build a consistent brand and reputation.

In addition, you should get involved with local projects and organizations whenever possible. You have learned how ENVE Composites supports biking events, trails, and bike paths in their hometown, and Mary DeLima provides free riding programs for disadvantaged children in her county. The more interaction you have with people in your own area, the more rewarding the service will be for you and your teammates. This is easy if you are building a geographical community but harder if you are building a niche community. However, you might support national organizations that have a main office or regional presence in your area. While it is great to send money to causes elsewhere in the world, that doesn't always bring you and your team members together in a community effort.

REFLECTION

Creating Your Community Strategy

The organizations we build can play a huge role in addressing the challenges we face in our communities. While we have a *responsibility* to do no harm, we also have a tremendous *opportunity* to make a real difference. I encourage all the aspiring entrepreneurs I work with to build a social component into their business plan from day one. At first, the contribution may be time, skills, and expertise. Later on it may include financial resources as well. Using business models to address community concerns provides great solutions to our challenges as well as tremendous benefits to our businesses. The questions below will help you create a sound and well-planned strategy for making a difference in your community.

1. What is your purpose and the brand you are trying to build in your community?
2. Based on your purpose, what are the values that are most important to you, your team members, and your organization?
3. What are five to ten key skills and core competencies that you, your team members, and your organization have to offer?
4. From the list of skills above, which ones are you and your team members most passionate about sharing with your community?
5. What are some potential nonprofits, charities, social organizations, or government offices in your community that may benefit from your company's involvement?
6. Select several organizations from your list above that you are most interested in supporting. Why is each a great match with your overall company brand?

EPILOGUE

Building Your Own New Enterprise

"The American Dream is still alive out there, and hard work will get you there. You don't necessarily need to have an Ivy League education or to have millions of dollars of startup money. It can be done with an idea, hard work, and determination."

—Bill Rancic, entrepreneur, author, winner of first season of *The Apprentice*

After completing our wild escapade across America, I was interviewed by a number of journalists. Many of them asked, "What is the most important thing you learned from this experience?" I always answered, "I strongly believe that anyone who wants to build a business can do it if they follow the key practices we have observed." I honestly believe this is true! Admittedly, not everyone can create game-changing technology, not everyone can secure venture capital, and not everyone can build a $50 million company. But everyone can build the kinds of Main Street businesses we saw all across the country. It doesn't take business genius, advanced training, a lot of money, an all-star cast, or sophisticated technology; it takes a powerful purpose, real-world experience, a variety of resources, people with passion and tenacity, and giving exceptional service. This approach has been used successfully for hundreds of years by every day men and women like you and me, long before there were humongous corporations.

The story of the Wright Brothers is a wonderful example from history of how these powerful principles allowed two unknown inventors to outperform a better-educated and better-funded competitor. While Orville and Wilbur were tinkering in their Ohio bicycle shop, Samuel Pierpont Langley was seriously striving to build the first airplane. At the time, Langley was the secretary of the Smithsonian Institution. He had taught mathematics and astronomy at Harvard, the Naval Academy, and the Western University of Pennsylvania. He had a spacious office, an attractive salary, a talented staff, powerful friends like Andrew Carnegie and Alexander Graham Bell, and $70,000 in funding, primarily from the War Department and the Smithsonian. This was a significant amount of money at the time (equivalent to $2 million today) to build a small one-passenger prototype, and the press followed him everywhere he went. After his prototype "Aerodrome" crashed twice in 1903 (the pilot escaped unscathed), Langley was ridiculed by the press and abandoned the project.

By contrast, Orville and Wilbur fell in love with the idea of flying. Their father gave them a toy helicopter when they were young; they played with it until it broke, and then they made their own. Although neither attended college, they were voracious readers who studied everything they could find about flying. With virtually no funding, they built a bicycle manufacturing company and used the earnings to fund their experiments in flight. While Samuel Langley focused on the design of the plane and the size of the motor (with four times more horsepower than the Wright Brothers' engine), Wilbur and Orville focused on the pilot's control of the aircraft. Their experience with bicycles taught them a great deal about controlling an unstable contraption. They believed that flying machines needed to turn, bank, and lean just like bicycles so the pilot could maintain equilibrium. They built their own wind tunnel to design their plane and developed a three-axis control system. While Samuel Langley's prototype cost nearly $70,000, the Wright Brothers' "Flyer" cost less than $1,000, paid for with proceeds from their bicycle business. On December 17,

1903, at Kitty Hawk, North Carolina, their plane flew 120 feet in 12 seconds at 6.8 miles per hour.

After their historic flight, the Wright Brothers continued to fly under the radar of the media. They were not working for fame and fortune; they were trying to open the skies to humankind. While subsequent years led to lawsuits, patent disputes, and questions about who was really the first to fly, the three-axis control system Wilbur and Orville created is still the standard for fixed-wing planes today.

The passionate work of the Wright Brothers gave birth to the multibillion-dollar aviation industry. Although Wilbur and Orville created their company more than 100 years ago, they followed the same principles I have seen used by hundreds of entrepreneurs—both those we visited on our tour across America and countless others I have interviewed. The Wright Brothers' story shows that better outcomes are achieved when entrepreneurs have a powerful purpose and follow the keys to success presented in this book. Table E–1 compares the practices of the Wright Brothers with those of Samuel Langley.

The Wright Brothers	Samuel Langley
Had a powerful driving purpose	Was paid a salary to do his job
Had relevant real-world experience	Had strong academic credentials
Had a passionate team of two	Had a paid staff of skilled experts
Shared findings with others	Kept all tests and findings secret
Maximized all available resources	Spent a lot of money on the project
Worked with a zealous tenacity	Did the job he was paid to do
Built an alternative revenue stream	Had significant funding sources
Worked for the good of humankind	Worked for fame and recognition
Learned and recovered from failure	Quit after several major failures

Table E–1: **The Wright Brothers vs. Samuel Langley**

Applying the Nine Key Practices

The nine practices highlighted in this book are the key "differences that make the difference" between success and failure when building a new enterprise. It's all about probabilities. The more the nine practices are applied in a new and growing venture, the greater the probability for success. The less these practices are present, the greater the chances for failure. These nine keys are summarized in Figure E–1. Notice how every key practice revolves around your "why" or purpose for starting your business. Once you have a powerful and engaging purpose, you cycle through the additional steps in the model. After completing the cycle once, most successful entrepreneurs repeat the

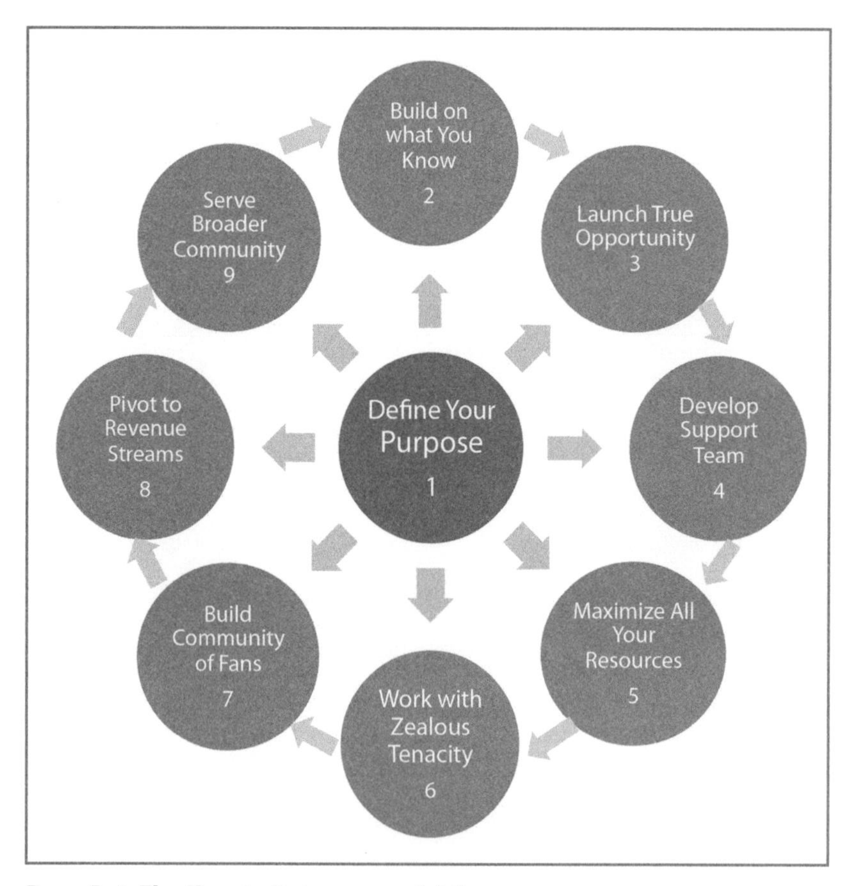

Figure E–1: **The Keys to Entrepreneurial Success**

process many times as they pivot to subsequent opportunities and revenue streams, always applying the same powerful keys to success with each new project.

Here's one more story that shows how all the pieces fit together. Ken and Vicki Stobbe have been building businesses in Newton, Kansas, for more than 30 years. They moved to Newton when Ken took a job as the laboratory director at the Newton Medical Center. Vicki worked for a group of attorneys the first three years, but when her second child was born, she decided she wasn't going back to work. She wanted more control over her life. She loved buying things, she loved helping people, and she wanted to create her own company (her driving purpose).

Vicki's mom had been a successful entrepreneur. She started a restaurant when she was 25 years old, then a coupon company, a consignment store, and a furniture business. Vicki worked with her from the time she was in high school and learned a great deal about running a company. Based on this experience, Vicki was confident she could build her own successful business in retailing (build on what you know). As she talked with friends and family members, she realized a gift store made sense because there was nothing like that in Newton. Vicki knew their town of 16,000 people could support the concept she had in mind (launch a true opportunity).

Vicki had great support from Ken and her parents. She also found team members who loved what she was doing and wanted to get involved. Much of her success has come from the strategic partnerships she has developed with manufacturers and sales reps, whom she has used again and again (develop your supporting cast):

> *Some people at market call me their mother. They say, 'Oh, Momma Stobbe is here.' That's a great feeling, that we have those relationships and can work together. If you can't work with them or they can't work with you, it is very, very difficult in this business. You have got to be loyal to them and they will be loyal to you.*

Vicki used a variety of resources to start her first business, High Street Company. She and Ken had some of their own funds, she obtained a small loan, and her parents helped buy the initial inventory. They opened the business in an old grocery store in town (maximize all resources). The business was profitable the first year, and Vicki paid back all the money she had borrowed.

Vicki raised her two children, Tina and Shawn, in the store. As they grew older, they became more and more helpful in the business. They worked hard as a family, loved serving customers, and enjoyed growing the business together (work with zealous tenacity). Here are some of their comments:

> Vicki: *I get a lot of fulfillment from being here on a daily basis, working a lot of hours to see who is coming in and what they are saying about us. Ken and I finally took a day away on a Saturday . . . but I could hardly stand not calling to find out: 'What's going on? Who's buying what? How are we doing?' I sometimes talk about retirement, but I don't know if I can do it because I just want to be here.*

> Tina: *It's been a dream of mine to open my own business ever since I was a little girl. . . . I didn't grow up in a house; I grew up in the store. I loved being there. I loved interacting with the customers. I even loved the behind-the-scenes stuff. I never wanted to do anything else. I just thought it was so fun to go to market and buy stuff, and to help people find the right gift.*

> Shawn: *One thing about these small businesses is you don't hire a custodian or maintenance guy. You are that person! You are also the accountant and the marketing man. So I would always follow my dad around and learn the tricks of the trade, anything from fixing leaks in a toilet to making fudge and all kinds of things.*

Building a strong community of loyal followers has been a major priority for the Stobbe family over the years. Here is how Vicki explains the philosophy that has helped them grow to where they are today (build a community of raving fans):

> *Our mission is to have that caring attitude with our customers. We know a lot of them by name because they come in on a weekly basis. We want to build relationships with them. We want to find out who*

> *they are and what they need. The better we know them, the more we can cater to them. Sometimes I say we should all have counseling degrees because they come in to talk with us. . . . If we don't take care of them, they can go down the road, and they can go to the internet. We don't even have to have the right merchandise, which I hope we always do, but people want to feel that we give them our time and energy and enthusiasm. People need hugs! So we become friends with them.*

One of the most interesting things the Stobbe family has done to stay viable over the past 30 years is to develop multiple streams of revenue. They started by adding more and more products to their initial store, High Street Company. What started as a gift shop grew into a diversified boutique and home décor business. They kept adding products and services based on input from suppliers and feedback from customers. After ten successful years, they opened Main Street Company, a card and paper products store on Main Street in Newton; they also bought a kitchen supply company, Kitchen Corner, and moved it right next to their card and paper business. Several years ago, they consolidated the merchandise from High Street Company into their two stores on Main Street, which lowered their operating overhead and put all their products and services in one central location. Today, Main Street Company is a boutique that sells sassy shoes, beautiful clothing, and gorgeous accessories. Kitchen Corner sells chef's tools, colorful linens, bakeware, pottery, tumblers, and fresh fudge made daily. Customers who visit their stores can shop for multiple products in one easy stop (pivot to multiple revenue streams).

In 2011, the family opened another store for Tina to run just 30 miles south of Newton in Wichita, which has fulfilled her dream of running her own company. Tina named the store in honor of her grandmother, who was such an influential mentor in her life. While they were brainstorming for a name, a red bird flew up and sat on their fence. Since her grandmother loved birds, Tina named the store the Red Bird Boutique. She has a picture of her grandmother in the store, and she uses her old desk. In addition, Shawn recently opened a

Dickey's Barbecue Pit just down the street from their two Main Street stores, where the lines are often out the door.

Finally, Vicki feels that getting involved in her community early on played a role in the success of her business. Since she was new in town and didn't know anyone, she joined the Chamber Board, the Children's Choir Board, and the Tourism Board, and supported carnivals and school activities. It's all part of building a community of raving fans (serve the broader community). While the Stobbes' ventures have been a lot of hard work, with the typical ups and downs of running an enterprise, they have taken control of their lives, are doing what they love, and enjoy working together as a family. Their story highlights the key practices for building a successful company.

Paying the Price for Success

Twenty years ago, my friend Kim Briggs and I helped our sons Eric and Chris earn the bicycling merit badge for their Eagle Scout Award. It required six short rides and then a 50-miler. After completing our 50-mile ride, none of us wanted to sit on anything smaller than a couch ever again. If you had told me I would ride my bike across America someday, I would have asked what you had been smoking. Now I can see that what it takes is careful planning, a lot of hard training, and perseverance. I truly believe that anyone who wants to do it can. It's simply a matter of paying the price.

Likewise, I believe anyone with a strong purpose can build a community-based business. It takes a true opportunity, a motivated team, a handful of resources, and a sincere commitment to building a community. Most of all, it takes sustained effort over time until traction is achieved and multiple revenue streams are established. Building a business is not for the faint of heart; it's not for anyone with a victim's mentality; and it's not for people who feel the world owes them a living. It requires taking responsibility for your life and working hard until your venture succeeds. Without a strong work ethic, it isn't going to happen. I am not a big fan of get-rich-quick schemes because I have never seen them work.

In his insightful book *The Outliers*, Malcom Gladwell introduces the concept of "10,000 hours." Using numerous examples, he shows that it takes roughly 10,000 hours of practice to become great in any field. For example, the Beatles performed for 10,000 hours in Hamburg, Germany, between 1962 and 1964 before they became international superstars. Bill Gates and Paul Allen each had 10,000 hours of programming experience before launching Microsoft. If you work 40 hours a week for 50 weeks a year, it will take five years to gain 10,000 hours of practice. If you work 60 hours a week for 50 weeks a year, it will take you a little more than three years. Thus, three to five years is the time commitment required to do anything great.

Three to five years is also the time frame most successful entrepreneurs say it takes to gain traction, produce positive cash flow, and build a sustainable company. So you can work for someone else for the next five years, or you can work for yourself. I think the latter is the better choice with the coming employment shift we are facing.

All the entrepreneurs we interviewed across the country believe the American Dream is still possible for anyone who is willing to pay the price for success. This doesn't mean the work is painful drudgery. Remember, successful entrepreneurs work hard to achieve a powerful purpose they believe in strongly. Thus, the hard work is a joyful experience the majority of the time, but it is required. Here are a few concluding thoughts from some of our role models.

> Julie Benson, cofounder of Energyneering: *I think we are definitely living the American Dream. We have horses in the backyard; we get to fly airplanes and do some really fun things. Not to say that we don't work hard because we do. People say, 'Why are you sending me emails at 2:30 A.M.?' Well, that's when I got to it [laughs]. We got a lot going on, but it's fun. It's all part of the lifestyle, and when you do something that you love, I think you'll succeed in the end. You just have to figure out what it is that you love.*

> Nicole Campos, founder of Bling: *If you work really hard, you can have the American Dream. . . . I will probably cry if I talk about it, but I always tell my husband that I wish our son could see*

where we came from to where we are at. With continued expansion, we hope to show him that all it takes is work. You just have to work really hard, and you can do whatever you want. I believe it; we're proof of it!

Steve Sullivan, founder of Stio: *I do think that the dream is alive and well. . . . It's being able to ski powder a hundred days a year [laughs]. It's being able to raise a family in a safe and comfortable environment. One of the great things about this country is that anyone can seek a good opportunity or start a business. So if you have a great idea and apply yourself, I think you can have the American Dream. I tell my kids this all the time and my mom used to say this so much, I think it is one of the reasons I became an entrepreneur: The world doesn't owe you a living! If you go out there and try, you can find your own dream.*

Patrick Hayden, founder of Kentucky Gun Co.: *I think I am about as close as I can get to the American Dream. . . . I guess my number-one piece of advice is, don't give up. The first two or three years are not going to make sense. I think the statistic is that most businesses fail within the first two or three years, so if you get past three, you are above average. I guess more importantly, don't let anybody tell you that you can't do something. I often use that as motivation to try a little harder and get something done.*

Allen Lim, founder of Skratch Labs: *I'm Chinese, but I was born in the Philippines. I grew up in Los Angeles in Chinatown, then East L.A., and then we worked our way out to the 'burbs. So I've seen the American Dream in my parents' lives and in what they wanted for us. I have seen it with respect to my education and the opportunity to start a business and support other people. I can't imagine anywhere else in the world where that possibility would have been available to me with my background. . . . But I realize the only way this happens is when you struggle for it; the best things in life are the things that you work hard for. In bicycle racing in the Tour de France, we had this saying called 'ninety-nine one.' Ninety-nine percent is all this work, suffering, and hardship. One percent is pure magic, and you live for the magic. There is nothing in the world you wouldn't do for that one little sliver of magic. So yeah, the American Dream is 'ninety-nine one.' That's what it is!"*

Polly Hinds, cofounder of Mad Dog and the Pilgrim Booksellers: *Every week we talk about, 'Man we should do blah-blah-blah, because we could just kick butt!' There are so many things you can do. I love history, I've studied it my whole life. I can tell you beyond a shadow of a doubt, there's never been a time that is better for women in this country than right now. If you want to start a business as a woman, it's the best place in the world to be. So the dream is still there!*

Creating Your Game Plan

As we discussed in the Prologue, we are on the verge of a major employment shift, as technology is eliminating jobs at an accelerated pace. Every year the software, computers, robots, and machines we create become more sophisticated and capable of doing a wide variety of jobs once held by humans. As a result, entire employment categories are being eliminated in nearly every industry. A host of studies predict that nearly half of our current jobs will become obsolete in the coming years, unemployment will rise significantly, and many of us will experience periods of financial insecurity.

I am more optimistic than some of the naysayers. We have faced major employment shifts in the past and come out of them just fine. In 1900, 41 percent of us worked in agriculture; today the number is 2 percent. Likewise, just after World War II, 30 percent of us worked in manufacturing; today the number is 10 percent. The important question now is whether we can keep up with the light-speed changes technology development will require. Some experts believe it will take longer to make the employment shift this time because jobs are being annihilated much faster than new industries are being created to replace those jobs.

Here is the all-important lesson: We need to be prepared for this employment shift to minimize its impact. While we don't know exactly what the jobs of the future will look like, we can count on more contract work, more project-based opportunities, more part-time employment, and shorter employment periods. This is why many experts are referring to the future as the new "gig" or "freelance" economy. The best way to navigate this new economy is to create our own jobs and build our own companies. Ironically, we can use the same technology that is destroying corporate jobs to live where we want, reach markets beyond our geographical location, and take advantage of the growing preference for smaller businesses over large corporations. The entrepreneurs we met all across the country have shown us how to do this by creating unique jobs for themselves and others in attractive places where there are no full-time jobs.

This new career model will require each of us to take full responsibility for our own future. We need to view ourselves as our own distinctive enterprise and develop the attitude and skills to succeed. We must learn how to identify critical needs in communities, develop products and services to meet those needs, build a strong supporting cast of team members, maximize all available resources, provide astounding value to customers, cultivate multiple revenue streams, and operate impressively in tight-knit communities. We might build one or more ventures, do contract work, and invest in real estate and other valuable assets. Here again in Figure E–2 on page 191 is the new career model we introduced in the Prologue for managing our changing economy.

REFLECTION

Building Your Dream Checklist

The final exercise starting on page 192 will help you assess how prepared you are on the nine keys to success introduced in this book. If you already have your own business, answer the questions to see where you can strengthen your company. Also complete the assessment before launching any new products, services, or opportunities.

If you are contemplating founding a new business, complete this exercise before launching your company. If you can answer "Yes" to

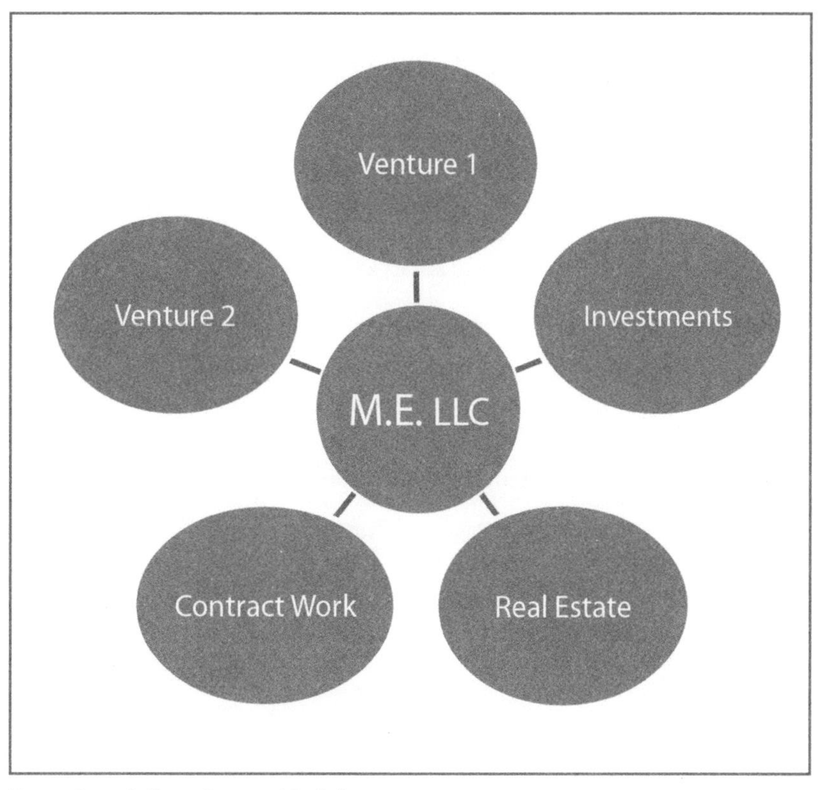

Figure E–2: **A New Career Model**

all these questions, you are ready to go. If not, simply take more time to prepare. You can also try answering the following questions about other opportunities you may be considering. The one with the most "Yes" answers will be your best bet.

I know you can take control of your future, create your own job, grow your own company, and enjoy the lifestyle of your dreams. It has been a pleasure sharing this book with you. I wish you the very best in your exhilarating career.

Step 1: Start with a Clear Purpose

	Yes	No
I have a clear and motivating purpose for starting my business.		
My purpose is powerful enough to pull me through difficult times.		
My purpose is engaging enough to attract key people to my venture.		

Step 2: Build on What You Know

	Yes	No
I have experience in the industry in which I am starting my business.		
I have experience in one or more industries related to my new business.		
I have personal experience with the products or services in this industry.		

Step 3: Launch Opportunities Not Ideas

	Yes	No
I have strong evidence that a need exists for my product or service.		
My skills and experience give me credibility to start my new venture.		
I have the resources I will need to start my new business.		
I have customers who are ready to buy my products right now.		
My business model for making money in this venture is sound.		

Step 4: Develop Your Supporting Cast

	Yes	No
I have a group of mentors and advisors who can help me build my business.		

	Yes	No
I know great potential team members who have or can learn the required skills.		
I have the strategic partners I will need to succeed in this venture long term.		

Step 5: Maximize All Available Resources

	Yes	No
I have many nonfinancial resources available to start my new venture.		
I know how and where to get other resources I will need to get started.		
I know how and where to get funding to grow when the time is right.		

Step 6: Work with a Zealous Tenacity

	Yes	No
I am very passionate about starting and growing my own business.		
I have the tenacity required to overcome all the challenges I will face.		
I know how to maintain my zealous tenacity over the long run.		

Step 7: Build a Community of Raving Fans

	Yes	No
I have identified the community of customers I want to reach.		
I have a plan for exceeding the expectations of my customers.		
I know how to include customers in the development of my business.		
I can create a system for maintaining mind-boggling service over time.		

Step 8: Pivot to Multiple Revenue Streams

	Yes	No
I have other products or services I can develop for my customer base.		
I am familiar with other market niches for my basic products and services.		
I know several other businesses I can create to use my resources.		

Step 9: Serve Your Broader Community

	Yes	No
I have identified several community initiatives I am passionate about.		
I know which projects are most consistent with my purpose and values.		
I am prepared to support an important project within my community of fans.		

Acknowledgments

This book would not have been possible without the untiring support from my team members who accompanied me on my ride across America: my remarkable wife, Mary Glauser; my savvy business partner, Shawn Sadowski; and my talented son, Jay Glauser. They found entrepreneurs, booked appointments, managed logistics, cheered me on, and allowed me to draft behind them on difficult days. I also want to thank our many backers on Kickstarter and the sponsors who provided funds and/or products for our journey: Adventure Cycling Association, Mass Mutual Intermountain West, Lendio, Max International, ENVE Composites, Sinclair Oil Corporation, Fezzari Bicycles, Skirt Sports, Boa Technology, Justin's, Skatch Labs, Bobo's Oat Bars, Lip'Shinin Marketing, Trusted Lube, Livliga, and Doc's Skin Care.

Special thanks to the many friends and associates who read earlier versions of my manuscript and provided invaluable feedback: Bob Henson, Natalie McCullough, Amy Bradford, Brandon Stoddard, Scott Hammond, Katherine McConkie, Joanne McCall, Mark Cook, Jaime Glauser, and my students at Utah State University. And thanks to my excellent colleagues in the Jon M. Huntsman School of Business who have encouraged and supported my work, especially Natalee Champlin,

Andy Thunell, Brayden Sparrow, James Davis, and Douglas Anderson, our exceptional dean.

I am grateful to the excellent editors I have had on this project: Michelle Martinez, Karen Billipp, and Wyn Hilty. The team at Entrepreneur Press has also been super: Jillian McTigue, who believed in the book, and Jennifer Dorsey, who brought it to fruition. The book would not have made it to such a great publisher without my extraordinary agent, Wendy Keller of Keller Media. I could not ask for a better partner in publishing and I hope this is the first of many projects together. Finally, a very heartfelt thanks to the many entrepreneurs who agreed to participate in this project. Meeting with them was one of the highlights of my career. The simple yet valuable concepts they teach can help all of us achieve the lifestyle of our dreams.

About the Author

Mike has extensive experience as an entrepreneur, business consultant, author, speaker, and university professor. He is the cofounder and chairman of My New Enterprise, an online training and development company for aspiring entrepreneurs and business builders. He has also built successful companies in the retail, wholesale, and consulting industries. Mike has worked with hundreds of startup companies and large corporations in the areas of product development, business strategy, organization effectiveness, and leadership development. His clients have included Associated Food Stores, The Boeing Company, Department of Workforce Services, Esso of Inter-America, Harmon Music Group, Jamberry Nails, Syntek Global, and USANA Health Sciences.

Mike is currently the Executive Director of the Jeffrey D. Clark Center for Entrepreneurship in the Jon M. Huntsman School of Business at Utah State University. He has designed and taught courses in business strategy, entrepreneurship, management, and organization development. He has published numerous articles in magazines and professional journals, and two previous books on entrepreneurship: *Glorious Accidents: How Everyday Americans Create Thriving Companies* and *The Business of Heart: How Everyday Americans are Changing the World*. Mike has appeared on Associated Press Radio, Voice of America, Good Morning Chicago, Great Day America, and First Business from Washington. He received a Ph.D. from Purdue University, and BS and MS degrees from the University of Utah.

References

Prologue

American Express Small Business Saturday. www.americanexpress.com/us/content/small-business/shop-small/about/.

Brynjolfsson, Erik, and Andrew McAfee. *Race Against the Machine: How the Digital Revolution Is Accelerating Innovation, Driving Productivity, and Irreversibly Transforming Employment and the Economy*. Boston: Digital Frontier Press, 2012.

Carr, Nicholas. *The Glass Cage: Automation and Us*. New York: W. W. Norton & Company, 2014.

Cohen, Patricia. "Middle Class, But Feeling Economically Insecure." *New York Times* (April 10, 2015). www.nytimes.com/2015/04/11/business/economy/middle-class-but-feeling-economically-insecure.html?_r=0.

Condon, Bernard, and Paul Wiseman. "AP Impact: Recession, Tech Kill Middle-Class Jobs." *Yahoo! News* (January 23, 2013). http://news.yahoo.com/ap-impact-recession-tech-kill-middle-class-jobs-051306434--finance.html.

Cox, Wendell. "America Is More Small Town than We Think." *NewGeography.com* (September 10, 2008). www.newgeography.com/content/00242-america-more-small-town-we-think.

Ford, Martin. *Rise of the Robots: Technology and the Threat of a Jobless Future*. New York: Basic Books, 2015.

Frey, Carl Benedikt, and Michael A. Osborne. "The Future of Employment: How Susceptible are Jobs to Computerisation?" University of Oxford (September 17, 2013). www.oxfordmartin.ox.ac.uk/downloads/academic/The_Future_of_Employment.pdf.

Goldman Sachs 10,000 Small Businesses. www.goldmansachs.com/citizenship/10000-small-businesses/US/index.html.

"Ideal Community Type." Pew Research Center (June 12, 2014). www.people-press.org/2014/06/12/ideal-community-type/.

Khazan, Olga. "More Americans Prefer Small Businesses to Large Companies, Survey Finds." *The Washington Post* (November 15, 2011). www.washingtonpost.com/blogs/on-small-business/post/more-americans-prefer-small-businesses-to-large-companies-survey-finds/2011/11/15/gIQAPrTqON_blog.html.

Luhby, Tami. "America: More Diverse, Less Wealthy." *CNN Money* (July 27, 2015). http://money.cnn.com/2015/07/27/news/economy/wealth-diverse/index.html?sr=twmoney072715americaispoorernoonstory.

McVeigh, Karen. "US Employers Slashing Worker Hours to Avoid Obamacare Insurance Mandate." *The Guardian* (September 30, 2013). www.theguardian.com/world/2013/sep/30/us-employers-slash-hours-avoid-obamacare.

Nisen, Max. "Robot Economy Could Cause Up to 75 Percent Unemployment." *Business Insider* (January 28, 2013). www.businessinsider.com/50-percent-unemployment-robot-economy-2013-1.

Rane, Neel, and Simon Frankel. "The Campaign Against Chains—Formula Retail in San Francisco." *CovBrands* (December 10, 2013).

www.covbrands.com/2013/12/10/the-campaign-against-chains-formula-retail-in-san-francisco/.

Rotman, David. "How Technology Is Destroying Jobs." *MIT Technology Review* (June 12, 2013). www.technologyreview.com/featuredstory/515926/how-technology-is-destroying-jobs/.

Schlaikjer, Erica. "City or Suburbs? Americans Want It Both Ways." *TheCityFix* (February 24, 2009). http://thecityfix.com/blog/city-or-suburbs-americans-want-it-both-ways/.

Tüzemen, Didem, and Jonathan Willis. "The Vanishing Middle: Job Polarization and Workers' Response to the Decline in Middle-Skill Jobs." *Economic Review* (First Quarter 2013). www.kansascityfed.org/publicat/econrev/pdf/13q1tuzemen-willis.pdf.

"What Americans Think About Business." Public Affairs Pulse Survey, Public Affairs Council (2011, 2012, 2013). http://pac.org/pulse/.

Yen, Hope. "4 in 5 in USA Face Near-Poverty, No Work." *USA Today* (September 17, 2013). www.usatoday.com/story/money/business/2013/07/28/americans-poverty-no-work/2594203/.

Chapter 1

"America's Historic Triangle." Colonial Williamsburg. www.history.org/foundation/historic_triangle.cfm.

"Frequently Asked Questions." SBA Office of Advocacy (March 2014). www.sba.gov/sites/default/files/FAQ_March_2014_0.pdf.

Gage, Deborah. "The Venture Capital Secret: 3 Out of 4 Start-Ups Fail." *The Wall Street Journal* (September 20, 2012). www.wsj.com/articles/SB10000872396390443720204578004980476429190.

Rao, Dileep. "Why 99.95% of Entrepreneurs Should Stop Wasting Time Seeking Venture Capital." *Forbes* (July 22, 2013). www.forbes.com/sites/dileeprao/2013/07/22/why-99-95-of-entrepreneurs-should-stop-wasting-time-seeking-venture-capital/.

Ride Oregon. http://rideoregonride.com/.

"TransAmerica Trail." Adventure Cycling Association. www.adventurecycling.org/routes-and-maps/adventure-cycling-route-network/transamerica-trail/.

U.S. Small Business Administration. www.sba.gov/.

"Yorktown Victory Monument: One Country—One Constitution—One Destiny." Yorktown. www.visitingyorktown.com/yorktown-monument.html.

Chapter 2

Craig, Nick, and Scott A. Snook. "From Purpose to Impact." *Harvard Business Review* (May 2014). https://hbr.org/2014/05/from-purpose-to-impact.

Frankl, Viktor E. *Man's Search for Meaning.* Boston: Beacon Press, 2006.

Horowitz, Sara. "Why Millennials Understand the Future of Work Better Than Anyone Else." *Fast Company* (April 1, 2015). www.fastcompany.com/3044478/the-future-of-work/why-millennials-understand-the-future-of-work-more-than-anyone-else.

"My New Enterprise Tour 2014." Kickstarter (May 2014). www.kickstarter.com/projects/1140205981/my-new-enterprise-tour-2014/description.

Raphelson, Samantha. "Amid the Stereotypes, Some Facts About Millennials." NPR.org (November 20, 2014). www.npr.org/2014/11/18/354196302/amid-the-stereotypes-some-facts-about-millennials.

Salzberg, Barry. "'I Am Millennial. Hear Me Roar!'" *Entrepreneur* (January 28, 2015). www.entrepreneur.com/article/242151.

Sinek, Simon. *Start with Why: How Great Leaders Inspire Everyone to Take Action.* New York: Portfolio, 2011.

Winfrey, Oprah. "What Oprah Knows For Sure About Finding Your Calling." *O, The Oprah Magazine* (November 2012). www.oprah.com/spirit/Oprah-on-Finding-Your-Calling-What-I-Know-For-Sure

Chapter 3

Altucher, James. *Choose Yourself: Be Happy, Make Millions, Live the Dream*. Nulkaba, Australia: Lioncrest Publishing, 2013.

"The Battle of White Bird Canyon: First Fight of the Nez Perce." *HistoryNet.com* (June 12, 2006). www.historynet.com/the-battle-of-white-bird-canyon-first-fight-of-the-nez-perce.htm.

"How Spanx Got Started." *Inc.* video with transcript (January 20, 2012). www.inc.com/sara-blakely/how-sara-blakley-started-spanx.html.

O'Connor, Clare. "Spanx Inventor Sara Blakely on Hustling Her Way to a Billion-Dollar Business." *Forbes* (October 21, 2014). www.forbes.com/sites/clareoconnor/2014/10/21/spanx-inventor-sara-blakely-on-hustling-her-way-to-a-billion-dollar-business/.

"Putting Your Butt on the Line Pays Off!" Spanx.com. www.spanx.com/about-us.

Chapter 4

Griffith, Erin. "Why Startups Fail, According to Their Founders." *Fortune* (September 25, 2014). http://fortune.com/2014/09/25/why-startups-fail-according-to-their-founders/.

Shane, Scott A. *The Illusions of Entrepreneurship: The Costly Myths That Entrepreneurs, Investors, and Policy Makers Live By*. New Haven: Yale University Press, 2008.

"Startup Business Failure Rate by Industry." Statistic Brain Research Institute (February 2015). www.statisticbrain.com/startup-failure-by-industry/.

Chapter 5

Burke, Edmund R. *Serious Cycling, 2nd ed.* Champaign, Illinois: Human Kinetics, 2002.

Gill, Victoria. "Fly Like a Bird: The V Formation Finally Explained." *BBC News* (January 16, 2014). www.bbc.com/news/science-environment-25736049.

Marcus, Jon. "Bike Skill: How to Draft." *Bicycling* (March 31, 2014). www.bicycling.com/training/bike-skills/bike-skill-how-draft.

Schulze, Eric. "Ask Smithsonian: Why Do Geese Fly in a V?" *Smithsonian.com* video. www.smithsonianmag.com/videos/category/3play_1/ask-smithsonian-v-formation/?no-ist.

"V Formation." Wikipedia. https://en.wikipedia.org/wiki/V_formation.

Chapter 6

Glauser, Michael J. "Getting More from Less." In *Glorious Accidents: How Everyday Americans Create Thriving Companies*, 229-236. Salt Lake City: Deseret Book Company, 1998.

Glauser, Michael J. "Giving Something Back." In *Glorious Accidents: How Everyday Americans Create Thriving Companies*, 297-309. Salt Lake City: Deseret Book Company, 1998.

"Global Market Size of Outsourced Services from 2000 to 2014 (in Billion U.S. Dollars)." Statista.com. www.statista.com/statistics/189788/global-outsourcing-market-size/.

International Reciprocal Trade Association. www.irta.com/.

Sinek, Simon. *Start with Why: How Great Leaders Inspire Everyone to Take Action.* New York: Portfolio, 2011.

Chapter 7

Adkins, Amy. "Majority of U.S. Employees Not Engaged Despite Gains in 2014." Gallup (January 28, 2015). www.gallup.com/

poll/181289/majority-employees-not-engaged-despite-gains-2014.aspx.

Davidson, Jacob. “This Is Why You Should Consider Dumping Your Traditional Job.” *Money* (July 1, 2015). http://time.com/money/3943374/independent-workers-job-happiness/.

Glauser, Michael J. “Radiating Zeal.” In *Glorious Accidents: How Everyday Americans Create Thriving Companies*, 107-108. Salt Lake City: Deseret Book Company, 1998.

“MBO Partners State of Independence in America 2015.” MBO Partners (September 29, 2015). www.mbopartners.com/state-of-independence.

Chapter 8

“Breaks Interstate Park.” Kentucky State Parks. http://parks.ky.gov/parks/recreationparks/breaks-interstate/default.aspx.

Logan, Dave, John King, and Halee Fischer-Wright. *Tribal Leadership: Leveraging Natural Groups to Build a Thriving Organization*. New York: HarperBusiness, 2008.

Chapter 9

Glauser, Michael J. “Notching It Upward and Onward.” In *Glorious Accidents: How Everyday Americans Create Thriving Companies*, 258-265. Salt Lake City: Deseret Book Company, 1998.

“Gravity.” Warner Bros. video. http://gravitymovie.warnerbros.com/#/home.

Chapter 10

De Tocqueville, Alexis. *Democracy in America*. Translated by Gerald E. Bevan. New York: Penguin Classics, 2003.

Delancey Street Foundation. http://delanceystreetfoundation.org/.

Erickson, Milton H. *A Teaching Seminar with Milton H. Erickson, M.D.* New York: Brunner/Mazel, 1980.

Glauser, Michael J. "Healing Our Afflicted." In *The Business of Heart: How Everyday Americans Are Changing the World*, 128-136. Salt Lake City: Deseret Book Company, 1999.

O'Hanlon, Bill. "Stories of Change and Possibility: The African Violet Queen." YouTube video. www.youtube.com/watch?v=M9sVg36PKQs.

"The Yorktown Campaign of 1781." George Washington's Mount Vernon. www.mountvernon.org/george-washington/the-revolutionary-war/the-yorktown-campaign/?gclid=CKGwtcrStcYCFYiCfgodQZAOYg.

Epilogue

Collin, Dan. "Trump to Bill: You're Hired!" CBS News (April 16, 2004). www.cbsnews.com/news/trump-to-bill-youre-hired/

Dimitri, Carolyn, Anne Effland, and Neilson Conklin. "The 20th Century Transformation of U.S. Agriculture and Farm Policy." *Economic Information Bulletin No. 3*, United States Department of Agriculture (June 2005). http://www.ers.usda.gov/media/259572/eib3_1_.pdf.

Friedman, Gerald. "The Rise of the Gig Economy." *Dollars & Sense* (March/April 2014). http://dollarsandsense.org/archives/2014/0314friedman.html.

Gladwell, Malcolm. *Outliers: The Story of Success.* New York: Back Bay Books, 2011.

Kaufman, Micha. "2015 Forecast: You'll Never Work the Same Way Again." *Forbes* (December 12, 2014). www.forbes.com/sites/michakaufman/2014/12/12/2015-forecast-youll-never-work-the-same-way-again/.

Kenny, Charles. "Why Factory Jobs Are Shrinking Everywhere." *Bloomberg Business* (April 28, 2014). www.bloomberg.com/bw/articles/2014-04-28/why-factory-jobs-are-shrinking-everywhere.

Lebergott, Stanley. "Wages and Working Conditions." *Library of Economics and Liberty* (2002). www.econlib.org/library/Enc1/WagesandWorkingConditions.html.

Lee, Marlene A., and Mark Mather. "U.S. Labor Force Trends." *Population Bulletin* (June 2008). www.prb.org/pdf08/63.2uslabor.pdf.

McCullough, David. *The Wright Brothers.* New York: Simon & Schuster, 2015.

Vlietstra, Katie. "The Independent Contractor in the New Freelance Economy." *Huffington Post* (June 24, 2015). www.huffingtonpost.com/katie-vlietstra/the-independent-contracto_b_7655412.html.

Wald, Jeff. "5 Predictions for the Freelance Economy in 2015." *Forbes* (November 24, 2014). www.forbes.com/sites/waldleventhal/2014/11/24/5-predictions-for-the-freelance-economy-in-2015/.

Index